The Book of Cathy

A SOUTH AFRICAN CHILDHOOD

Catherine Kentridge

TO MY DEAREST REN

CONTENTS

ACKNOWLEDGMENTS

Dearest Dad, thank you for being willing to read the manuscript and to limiting yourself, on the whole, to factual corrections. Thank you for being open to reading my view of my childhood, although that view contained many surprises for you.

FOREWORD

The Book of Cathy is a memoir of my childhood in South Africa. I wanted to write about an ordinary white, middle class upbringing to balance the books written from very different experiences and perspectives about the South Africa of the 1950s and 1960s.

I grew up in these apartheid years, a privileged girl who lived in a big house with a big garden in a beautiful suburb, waited on by servants.

I have chosen not to put my childhood into its political context, since that context was the one in which I lived and that I took for granted, while aware that it was unjust and unconscionable. This awareness came from both parents, lawyers who fought for the rights, so restricted, of all the disenfranchised, then referred to as "non-whites." I bring politics into my memoir only if it impacted me directly, such as seeing election posters advertising, "Vote Liberal, if you

AGED ABOUT TWO

want a black man living next door!" or "Be a man not a mouse, vote for Gita Dysenhaus," or being drummed in to stuff envelopes with election flyers for the Liberals.

I also chose not to write the book from the point of view of now, as an older and wiser Cathy looking over her shoulder and saying, "Little did she know," or "That was just two months before the law making it a criminal offence to marry someone of a different race came into effect." There are

1

more than enough well-researched and illuminating books written by members of my generation and background in this style and viewpoint. Instead, I have attempted to write about life the way I experienced it at the time.

Most of all, I wanted to evoke my childhood in South Africa as vividly as I could for my Canadian-born daughter. The idea expanded and I found I wanted to create my own piece of the multi-coloured and multi-faceted tapestry of South Africa in the apartheid years.

I chose to write about memories by topic, not in chronological order, when I found this is how my memory worked best. One image triggered another, which triggered the next. Not being tied to chronology saved me the fruitless and frustrating exercise of wondering, "Did that happen when I was five or when I was six?" At any moment, while I was working on the manuscript, something seen, heard, read, smelled, or tasted might spark a memory to glitter briefly, yet brightly. I had to drop everything and rush to the computer to record it before it flickered and vanished forever.

To evoke the atmosphere more vividly, I have taken some licence with the words I put into people's mouths. The memories, the places, the voices, the sounds, the smells, and the tastes are all so strong. My aim is to capture the intense flavours and textures evocative of the times, as tasted in my mouth and as seen through my eyes.

Some of the language used in this memoir to refer to people of colour is not at all politically correct. I use it because that was the language in use at the time.

Catherine Kentridge
Toronto, Canada

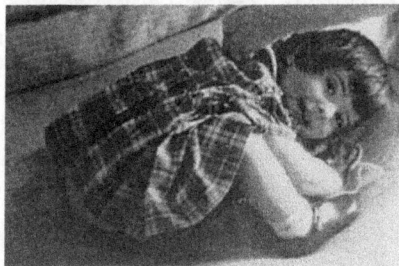

1—ELLEN AND JOHN

When I was very small, about three or four years old, I did something to annoy my nanny, Ellen, and she smacked me. I ran crying to John, the old gardener, who smoked dagga and lived in the windowless cellar beneath the house at Number 2 St. John's Road. He came flying to my rescue and stood shouting at Ellen, with his hands on his hips, "Why you smack the chile? You must not smack the chile!"

And I immediately stopped being afraid of him even though he smelled of dagga, and some of his front teeth were missing, and he seemed so very old and wrinkled with his hair so grey.

Usually, it was Ellen who comforted me when I was feeling sad, or hurt, or lonely. She would tell me what the cat said to the bird in the syringa tree. He cocked his head on one side and pleaded in his sweetest voice, "Mare-ree, please come down, Mare-ree, please come down."

The dove, on its branch, replied, "I've-got-nothing-to-do-with-you! I've got-nothing-to-do-with you!"

Yet, sometimes, I didn't like it when Ellen tried to tell me what to do or to forbid me to do anything I'd set my heart on.

One day at Plettenberg Bay, where we went for summer holidays, Ellen forbade me to wade into the sea above my knees. I was furious. "You think you're the prime minister of the whole world!"

Ellen's cooking was the best in the world, whether she was making lamb stew, cheese scones, chocolate cake, or the thin layers of nut-meringues

PHOTOGRAPH—CATHY, AGED ABOUT TWO

3

sandwiched together with coffee-cream for Madam and Master's dinner parties. (My mother was Madam and my father was Master.)

"Ellen, please can I help you in the kitchen today?" I would ask, at least twice a week. The kitchen was behind the dining room and had windows looking onto the back yard paved with concrete blocks. Around the back yard were the servants' quarters, small rooms with one window each, and the servants' bathroom, and the laundry room. The stove stood in an alcove that had once had a fireplace or perhaps a wood-and-coal-burning stove. The walls were covered in wallpaper with yellow sunflowers on it. There were green linoleum tiles on the floor, and a counter where Ellen mixed and rolled the dough and the pastry for her baking. Underneath the counter, Ellen kept the flour in tin-lined drawers so the mice could not get at it. But the tin did not keep out the weevils. Sometimes when we were just about to start mixing, we would see something move in the flour. "Ugh! There's a weevil," I yelled, and we had to throw out the whole container of flour and open a new bag.

"Let me see if your arms are strong enough to stir this dough." Ellen would put a big wooden spoon into my hand, and I'd stand on a sturdy wooden kitchen chair, gripping the spoon and stirring the dough for the bread rolls for a lunch party. After two or three turns around the bowl, my arm would ache.

"Miss Cathy, you are very weak. You must play more tennis to get strong arms."

I would try again, but my arms just ached and ached. I let Ellen finish the stirring and kneading. As compensation, I was allowed to shape the dough when it was ready for the bread tins and brush egg yolk mixture over the top, so the bread would be shiny when it came out of the oven.

Ellen usually allowed me to shell the peas that would be cooked for the grownups. "If you help me a lot, I will let you have some meringue before John brings it in to the guests. But you must fill the bowl with peas first. And then peel the grapes," said Ellen, as I sat down at the kitchen table.

"But I wanted to make the melon into balls," I'd complain.

"It's William's turn to do that."

"It's not fair. He always does them. You promised that I could do them today." I darted a furious look at William, who simply smiled at me.

2—THE GREEN SCHOOL

When I was three, I taught my nursery school teachers to swear. The school was part of the Teachers' Training College and it was on Duff Road, just across the street from my first home at Number 2 St. John's Road.

One morning, one of the children did something that annoyed me.

"Go away you bloody ox!" I yelled.

No one knew where I had heard this expression, pronounced *Bladdy Ox*. But the teachers loved it. Within days, they were cheerfully calling each other "You Bladdy Ox."

My nursery school was called The Green School. There were two other nursery schools, The Blue School and The Brown School. But who would want to go to a place called The Brown School?

The best thing about The Green School was graduating to *The Fives' Corner* when you reached the magic age of five. The Fives' Corner had all the best toys, puzzles, and books. When you sat in The Fives' Corner, all the younger children peered in enviously.

But there was something awful about The Green School—the Friday picnic. We'd sit outside in a circle, each on a little rubber mat. The food was always the same, cold *boerewors* and hard-boiled eggs. I could not bear eggs. As soon as I was sure the teachers weren't looking, I rolled my egg down the hill behind me so I would not have to eat it. Or I put it under my mat and sat on it.

Ellen had a word for my behaviour with food. "Miss Cathy, you're full of fiemies."

CATHY (IN A TARTAN PINAFORE MADE BY MAY) AND WILLIAM.

There was also something very strange that happened at The Green School. One morning I arrived at school ready to go and play in The Fives' Corner, as usual. But the principal, Miss Hallet, called me aside. "Cathy, we're going to test what kind of dreams you have." In her office were some grownups in white coats with smiles I didn't trust.

"But..."

"Don't be scared. We're going to put some sticky stuff on your head and then glue some wires onto it. Then you can close your eyes and tell us what you are dreaming about."

One of the people in a white coat smiled at me. "Your dreams will be in very bright colours. It will be fun."

I nodded uncertainly, very scared when I saw the wires and the machine. The sticky stuff had a funny smell and felt horrible on my head. I wondered how I would get it off, and if it would pull out chunks of hair when I tried. I began to cry. I don't know if I dozed off when the machine with its deep buzz that hummed in my head started up. But I know that I didn't dream at all.

The school reports said, "Cathy is a very friendly, clever child. And she is very good at telling stories. She is popular, even though she has a bit of a temper. She sets an example to the other children by how good she is at eating cabbage." But there was no mention of the brain tests. I never discovered the purpose of them or the results.

3—GRANDPARENTS

I had two complete sets of grandparents until I was 11. That's when my father's father, Morris, died at the age of 84. We grandchildren, who were 11, nine, two, and two-months-old at the time, did not attend the funeral.

Our maternal grandparents, Irene and Max, were known by everyone, not just the grandchildren, as 'Ga and Grampa'. My father's parents were 'May and Morris'.

Morris had always seemed immeasurably ancient. He was almost bald, with a thin rim of white hair, a hearing aid, and black-rimmed pince-nez glasses perched on the end of his nose. He wore a double-breasted suit. Morris was 20 years older than my grandmother, May, whom he married when she was 20 and he was 40. Morris had never learned to drive and May had always been their chauffeur.

GA, MY MOTHER'S MOTHER, IRENE GEFFEN, AND MAY, MY FATHER'S MOTHER, MAY KENTRIDGE, OUTSIDE THE MARYMOUNT NURSING HOME AFTER THE BIRTH OF WILLIAM IN APRIL, 1955

She drove Morris to visit us at Number 2 St. John's Road in her smart grey Citroen, with the running boards at the side. Later on, when we lived at Number 72 Houghton Drive, May had a grey Morris Minor that had to work very hard to get up the drive. We never knew if it would reach the top, or just give up and slide down to the bottom.

When I was very young, May told me that Morris did not like cats. "Cathy, it is your job to keep the cats away from Morris." This was an important job as our house had many cats.

So as soon as he arrived at Number 2 St. John's Road, and was sitting in a comfortable chair in the living room, I ran to close the door, after first checking that there were no cats in the room.

THE BEAUTIFUL PHOTOGRAPH OF MAY AND MORRIS ON THEIR WEDDING DAY, JANUARY 4, 1921, THAT HUNG IN MAY'S BEDROOM

Morris's voice always seemed to be full of phlegm and politeness. At the dinner table, he would ask, politely, "Could I trouble you to pass the salt?"

Morris had written his memoirs when he was in his 70s and gave an autographed copy to each of his grandchildren. He had been a well-known politician, and the walls of Morris and May's flat were covered in framed cartoons of Morris by famous political cartoonists such as Bob Connolly. These had appeared in the local papers over the years. They always emphasized the large nose, the monocle, and the striped double-breasted suit.

When Morris was very ill, he lived for a while in our house. I had to move out of my bedroom, so he could have it. Whenever I came into the room to visit him, I found strange and upsetting things in it. A large wooden chair with a potty underneath the seat, and stink coming from it, and on the bedside table a plastic bottle for peeing into, and a strong smell of old age and illness.

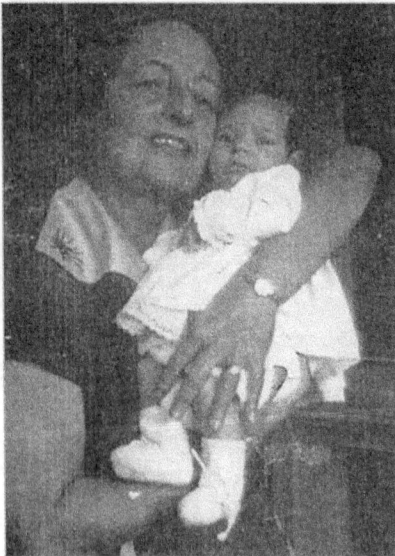

MAY WITH HER BRAND NEW AND FIRST GRANDDAUGHTER, CATHERINE EMMA HELEN

It was well-known by us children that when I was born—I was her first grandchild—May decided that she did not want to be called *Granny* or any form of it, because, "It will make me feel too old." Instead, she decreed that she was to be called "May" and my grandfather was to be "Morris."

May and I lived in a state of armed truce most of the time. Sometimes this erupted into open warfare or became a battle of silence. We had the same kind of tempers, both boiling over quickly into furious shouting matches. But we were also very different. I would explode with anger, then just as quickly cool down and want to apologize and be friends again. But not May.

Once, without thinking, I called out "Goodbye, Old Girl" as she was leaving. "Old Girl" was the secret name Ellen and I use to refer to May in private. May was enraged. She stewed over this insult, tenderly nursing and hoarding a grudge, and sent me to Coventry for two weeks. When she came to the house during this time, she made a great show of refusing to acknowledge my existence, talking over and around me and ignoring any word I addressed to her, giving hugs to my brothers and sister, and turning away from me.

GRAMPA AND GA, AS THEY STILL LOOK IN MY MEMORY.

May was a very good cook. However, for some reason, she did not wish to share her recipes with me, not even for her famous mandelbrot and her almond tart, which I loved. I had no desire either to eat or know the recipes for the cakes May seasoned with caraway seeds, which were fine in rye bread but had no place in sweet cakes or pastries. Nor did I wish to learn how to cook tongue, one of her favourite dishes. It made me sick just to think about, and the sight of tongue on the sideboard for Sunday lunch sent me running from the dining room.

However, when we were getting along, May would arrive with

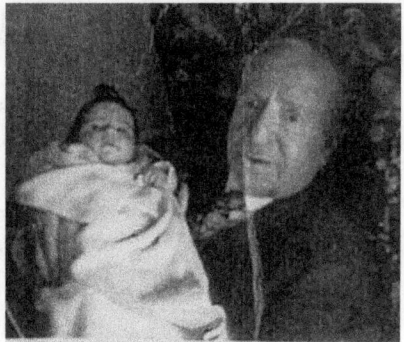

MORRIS WITH HIS BRAND NEW AND FIRST GRANDDAUGHTER, CATHY.

delicious things she had baked for me, or a new cardigan, pullover, dressing gown, or dress—always navy-blue or red. There were three things she sewed for me that I loved more than all the other homemade clothes and jerseys. I felt so pretty when I wore them. These were the red gingham skirt and blouse with broderie anglaise and a black ribbon through the lace at the neck, sleeves, and hem, and the red flannel dressing gown, lined with red with tiny white polka dots, and one pocket with lace edging. This was the snuggest and prettiest dressing gown ever. I wore all three until they were ragged and frayed, and I could not possibly fit into them any more

May was also a weaver and wove colourful, but itchy, wool bedspreads for our beds. William's was bright orange, blue, green, and yellow. Mine had pale pastel pinks, blues, greens, and yellows. May also wove rugs on a huge wooden loom. The rugs glowed in passages, living rooms, and bedrooms in our house.

When I visited May in her flat, I took a deep breath and inhaled the smell of cigarettes. May was a chain smoker. She tried and tried to give it up, or to smoke less. She would cut her cigarettes in half to smoke in a long black holder with a gold mouthpiece. But we were all sure she still smoked the same amount. It was just more of a nuisance to constantly light the cut cigarettes, the new one from the *stompie* of the old. Her copper ashtrays overflowed.

May loved to play bridge. She was a very good player and was always having bridge parties. She kept hard, wrapped sweets in little dishes left over from, or ready for, the regular games of bridge, and a bowl of cents ready for bets. She could shuffle cards so fast, all you saw was a blur of blue and red shapes rushing between her long red fingernails. And you heard the sounds of her copper bangles jingling, and the clink of the large rings on her fingers.

In May's bedroom, on top of the hautboy, she kept photographs of her wedding day. She was extremely pretty and wore what looked like harem pants and a flowing top. Her hair was cut in short soft waves, and she wore white shoes with little straps and low heels. She looked as glamorous as a film star. Her wedding clothes had come all the way from Paris. Morris wore a dark double-breasted suit, a monocle, and a top hat.

My favourite thing in the flat was a small copper iron, from the olden days when it would have been heated on the stove or over the fire, to iron clothes.

"May, can I iron your handkerchiefs and napkins?"

"Yes. But be sure not to burn them! Don't let the iron get too hot!"

The flat also contained a gloomy bronze bust of Morris. I tried not to see it as it gave me the creeps with its blind and hollow eye sockets.

When I was older, May came to look after us while my parents were overseas. One Saturday evening we got into a raging argument about my wanting to go out on a date with a boyfriend, who had been previously approved by my parents. May absolutely refused to allow me to go. Our voices got louder and we ended up screaming at each other.

"You are going to give me a HEART attack!" yelled May.

"I don't care. You're so horrible, I hate you!" I yelled back.

**

Poor darling Grampa, Max Geffen, my mother's father, loved his grandchildren so much, and we loved him very much, but he did not get much respect from us. We liked to tease him, and sometimes to shout at or argue with him.

Grampa says—
"A birdie with a yellow bill
Hopped upon my windowsill
Cocked his shiny eye and said,
'Wake up! Wake up! You sleepy head!'"

"It was a cold and frosty night
A man stood in the street
His aged eyes were full of tears,
And his boots were full of …. FEET!"

Grampa sings—
"Oh it's nice to get up in the morning
When the sun begins to shine
At four at five at six o'clock
In the good old summer time.
But when the snow is snowing and it's murky overhead
Oh it's nice to get up in the morning
But it's nicer to lie in bed!"

Grampa says, *"Tempus Fugit"* to get me and William to hurry along in the morning, finish our breakfast, and jump into the car to be driven to school. Grampa drove me to school almost every single day from when I began 'big school' in Grade one, aged six, until I finished Matric at 17.

Grampa writes in my pink leather autograph book,
"Lives of Great Men all remind us
We can make our lives sublime
And departing leave behind us
Footsteps in the Sands of Time."

GA AT MOM'S WEDDING, JANUARY 15, 1952.

Grampa loved to make up and recite doggerel, which we grandchildren referred to as "Grampa's rubbisherel."

Grampa was born to be a teacher. How I wished he could have been one of mine. He helped me with maths and science homework and was the only person who could make me understand algebra, geometry, and trigonometry. When he gave practical examples of when, how, and why to use these subjects, I began to accept they had not been created on purpose to torment my unmathematical brain.

"If you understand trig, you can make sure that the house you are building will not fall down," he said, scribbling a diagram with the pencil held awkwardly in his right hand.

"Grampa, I think I get my terrible handwriting from you."

"Well, Lovey, I was forced to write with my right hand, even though I am naturally left-handed, because being left-handed was forbidden when I was a child."

Grampa had been a teacher before he became an attorney.

"Grampa, why can't you be my maths teacher instead of Madam at Rodean?"

"Lovey, I wish I could. I became an attorney because I had to, not because I wanted to. I couldn't support a family on a teacher's salary. I would much rather have stayed being a teacher."

His law firm was called M&I Geffen, for Max and Irene Geffen. But it was really only Grampa in an office with an 'office boy' to run errands. Although Ga, my grandmother Irene, qualified as an attorney, she never practised.

Grampa's office had large grey filing cabinets and shelves filled with volumes of old Law Reports. There was a pungent smell of the fluid you put in to the Roneo. This was the copying machine. Documents came out on flimsy paper in purple ink. Grampa was very proud of it. He loved technology. He was the first person I knew who had an electric calculator, the first person to have a quartz watch, and the first person to drive a car with automatic gears, like they did in America. He was keen to pass on this love of technology to us, so on our birthdays he often gave us watches or calculators.

On Friday nights we had supper at Ga's house. Ga never said much on these occasions. She didn't come to schul with us—lucky Ga, we always thought—but waited at the flat for us to return. She never said much because Grampa would not let her.

"Oh, Irene, shut up," or "Nonsense, Irene," he'd say whenever she tried to say anything. Or he'd just interrupt her in the middle of a sentence.

I didn't like this at all. As I grew older, I'd shout at Grampa. "Let Ga finish what she is saying. I want to hear what she thinks."

Then Grampa would be angry with me for being disrespectful. I found it all very confusing, trying to work out how Grampa felt about Ga and why he treated her in this way. Because after shouting Ga down and causing her to leave the room, Grampa would turn to me and William and say, "Loveys, do you know Ga was the first woman in South Africa to qualify as an attorney? She got the gold medal for French at Wits University. She went to London to the London School of Economics for a year on a scholarship when she was only 21."

"Then why won't you let her speak?" I'd say.

No answer. He'd just start talking about something else, such as our favourite radio show.

"Who did you think should have been tonight's "Stars of Tomorrow?""

Apart from seeing Grampa every day when he drove me and William to school, and on the Friday evenings when we had supper at his flat, we often saw Ga and Grampa at weekends. On Sunday mornings, they arrived to fetch us and our cousins, Oliver and Lucy, who lived just up the road, for special treats.

"Where shall we go today?" said Grampa.

"To the Doll's House," said Oliver.

"To the aerodrome to watch the planes," begged William.

"To the zoo," I said.

Lucy said nothing.

Sometimes, I was lucky. For me, the best treat of all was the Johannesburg Zoo. Grampa would park his car in the parking lot and then he and Ga and the grandchildren would walk together up to the ticket booth, buy six tickets, and squeeze through the turnstile.

Grampa gave us each 25 cents to buy snacks. The first stop was the kiosk where you could buy monkey nuts in the shell to feed the monkeys, in their small, smelly side-by-side concrete cages. Their red raw bottoms were disgusting, but I couldn't stop looking at them; and I laughed at the way they searched for fleas in each other's fur.

Then we would lead Ga and Grampa to the place where you lined up for rides on the pony or a ride in the ponycart with the striped canopy, or on the back of an elephant. To get on, we climbed up a ladder, with someone holding tight to make sure we did not fall off.

Of course, this was all hungry and thirsty work, so it was often followed by a visit to the zoo café where you could drink red fizzy lemonade and eat ice-cream; and, perhaps, if you were extra good, or nagged long enough and hard enough, Grampa would buy you some of the wonderful, melt-in-the-mouth pink or bright green sticky candy floss. On Red Letter Days, Grampa might also buy you a lucky packet, which you always hoped would contain a shiny gold ring with a brightly-coloured stone mixed in amongst the hard sweets. Often, the only thing that was hidden among the sweets was a piece of paper with a fortune on it and a plastic whistle that broke at the first blow, or a tiny piece of red cellophane in the shape of a fish that curled up in your palm to show how you were feeling.

After the zoo café, we'd visit the polar bears in their dank, dark cage, or the elephants, outdoors in their dusty enclosures, or the hippos in their slimy pool. Peacocks called raucously from the trees along the paved pathways.

Sometimes, the Sunday trip would be to the Zoo Lake, where you could feed the ducks, have lunch at the café, or go for a row on the lake.

On some Sundays, we went all the way to Pretoria. This was a much longer expedition. Pretoria was at least 50 km from Johannesburg and there was no highway, only the old Pretoria Road.

We'd usually stop to visit the hideously ugly *Voortrekker* Monument on Pretoria's outskirts. It commemorated the people who had been in the Great Treks, all those people whose names we had to memorise for history tests. None of us liked this monument, which could be seen for miles in every direction. Its squat sides were covered with sculptures of Voortrekkers. The women wore sunbonnets, long dresses, and *veldskoen*; the men wore baggy trousers, hide hats, and *veldskoen*, and clutched their guns, surrounded by their oxen and their *ossewaen*.

A trip to Pretoria might also include a stop at Jan Smuts's house, where solemn guides would proudly show us evidence of the great man's austere lifestyle—his narrow cot in the small, sparsely furnished bedroom of the small, sparsely furnished little house. It was clear that austerity was pretty close to heroism or sainthood, and we know that Jan Smuts, soldier, commando leader, and politician, was a South African and a British hero.

Paul Kruger was another hero, an Afrikaner hero, a farmer, soldier, and builder of the Afrikaner nation. Sometimes, on the Pretoria visits, Grampa and Ga took us to see Paul Kruger's house. '*Oom* Paul's' house was a more impressive building, but very dark and formal.

Jan Smuts and Oom Paul were people we had to learn about in history lessons every single year.

On our way to or from Pretoria, we sometimes drove past a little town called 'Irene'. We were thrilled to see a place with the same name as Ga's. But if we blinked or happened to be looking the other way, we missed it; it was such a small place.

When William got his wish, Ga and Grampa drove us to the aerodrome, at Jan Smuts Airport. To get there we drove along busy main roads, past houses perched on the hills, along winding roads, and then out past the place where factories sent great clouds of smoke into the blue sky. These were the fizzy drinks factory and, best of all, the Simba Chips factory We always knew when they were making a big batch of roast-chicken-flavoured chips.

At Jan Smuts Airport, we went up the stairs to the viewing gallery to watch the planes taking off and landing and to dream of going somewhere far away in one of them. Grampa explained about all the different kinds of planes. He had wanted to be a pilot in the war, but was told that he was too old for active combat. So he'd stayed in South Africa working in something to do with aeroplanes and the war, but not actually flying anywhere. There were photos of him as an army officer, in his khaki uniform, with his swagger stick and his back held very straight and his chest puffed out. Of course, we always had fizzy drinks, sweets, and chips while we watched the planes.

When there wasn't time for big expeditions, or when no one was in the mood for looking at things, Ga and Grampa took us to the Dolls' House Drive-In Eatery. You drove a long way along Louis Botha Avenue till you came to the red sign. Then you drove into the parking lot and rolled down all the windows in the car. Then you hooted and a waitress ran over to take your order.

"Chips and a hamburger and strawberry milk shake for me, please," said William.

"Can I have a chocolate milkshake and just chips, no burger, please," I said.

When the waitress returned with the orders, she clipped a tray onto each window. We'd sit, eating and drinking and slurping our milkshakes to get the last drop, and thinking that nothing had ever tasted more delicious.

Even when Ga and Grampa were simply coming over for lunch or tea at our house, they never arrived empty-handed. Ga's bag always held a packet of Sugus, an Aero or a Flakey chocolate bar, or a box of Liquorice Allsorts. My mother would roll her eyes and remind us to brush our teeth after the sweets and say, "Mom, I've asked you not to bring them sweets every time. You'll ruin their teeth."

Ga would smile and look down.

My mother preferred the presents Grampa gave us on our birthdays, in addition to the watches or calculators. These were share certificates for South African Growth Equities. These could be guaranteed not to rot your teeth, not be consumed all at once, and to be of some benefit in the future.

4—CATS AND DOGS

Dad was driving. Mom was sitting beside him. William and I were in the back seat, very excited because we were on the way to get a new kitten. William and I were arguing.

"If it's a boy, he must be called Stanley," said William.

"Ugh, what a nasty name. If it's a boy, he must be called Socrates. We can call him Soxy for short. If it's a girl we can call her Jasmine."

"Those are stupid names. No cat would want those names."

"Be quiet you two or I'm turning the car around," Dad said from the front, without turning his head.

When we got to Barbara's house and she showed us the kittens, we forgot all our disagreements about names. There were three kittens. Mom had made sure we knew, before we got into the car, that we could only bring home one kitten. But which one? One kitten was grey and fluffy, the second had stripes, and the third was black with tiny bits of white on its throat and the tips of its paws.

William wanted the black kitten. I wanted the striped. Dad said the only fair thing to do was to toss a coin.

"Heads I win, tails you lose," shouted William, as Dad tossed the coin.

"That's not fair! I call heads."

It landed on tails, so we took the black kitten home, taking turns to cradle it in our arms. Barbara had lifted up its tail and said it was a boy.

Dad said that seeing William had the kitten he wanted, I could have the name I wanted—Socrates.

As soon as we got home, I rushed into the kitchen.

"Ellen, I need some butter for the kitten."

Ellen took some from the fridge. William held the kitten while I smeared butter on its paws, so it wouldn't be able to find its way back to its old home and would stay with us.

The kitten licked its paws carefully and thoroughly, and stayed with us for 10 years.

**

When I was about eight, we had another cat. Her name was Fran. She had golden eyes. I noticed that she was getting very fat. Her belly hung down and I could see her teats, especially when she lay on her back. I wondered how many kittens were in her tummy.

When she began to prowl around the house one evening, I knew what that meant. She was about to have her kittens and was looking for somewhere snug and hidden to have them. She went into William's room and didn't see anywhere she liked. Then she wandered, meowing, into Mom and Dad's room. There was an open door to the dark cupboard where Dad kept his shirts, but Ellen shooed her out of there.

I wanted Fran to have her kittens in *my* room so I picked her up carefully and brought her in. She inspected various open drawers and cupboards and then crept under the bed. But I didn't think it would be very nice for her to have her kittens under there, so I made a hiding place beneath my desk. I lined a large shallow cardboard box with an old towel and a soft piece of blanket, and borrowed a tablecloth from the linen cupboard to cover the desk. The cloth hung down to the floor like a curtain. I showed Fran her cubbyhole and she seemed to like it. She crept into the box.

When it was bedtime, I was half afraid to go to sleep. What if Fran had the kittens while I was sleeping? What if she didn't?

In the middle of the night, I awoke to strange meowing sounds coming from the darkness. I strained my eyes to see where the noise was coming from. I was too scared to get out of bed or turn on the light. Perhaps there would be blood and all kinds of muck that I didn't want to see.

I went back to sleep with my eyes screwed shut.

In the morning, five new, tiny, bald and blind kittens were in the box under the desk, and Fran was licking each face in turn, looking very pleased with herself.

Then the fun began. We had to keep Bimbo, our crazy allsorts dog, away from the kittens as I was convinced he would eat them. We moved Fran and her babies into the playroom, along with a litter box and plenty of food and milk. Bimbo knew at once that there was something very interesting behind the closed playroom door. He parked himself outside it, whining and sniffling, and tried to get into the room every time the door opened. I shrieked and shooed him away.

Meanwhile, the kittens grew. They opened their eyes and became furry and fluffy, climbing everywhere in the playroom. I found them sleeping in the toy box, or my dolls' laps, behind William's box of paints, or in the cupboards under the windows that looked onto the drive.

When the kittens were about three months old, Mom put her foot down. "Those cats can't stay in the playroom anymore. The room is getting very smelly. Those kittens need fresh air and they have to meet Bimbo."

I cried and cried. "They're too small. He'll eat them. He'll kill them. I *know* he will!"

"Don't be silly. We'll keep very close watch over the kittens and Bimbo."

So the kittens were carried downstairs in their basket, with Fran following anxiously behind.

On the front lawn, Bimbo waited, trembling with excitement. I put the basket onto the grass. I could hardly see for crying. Bimbo rushed over to the basket and picked up one of the kittens in his mouth.

I screamed. "Look. He's going to break its neck. I told you and told you not to let him near the kittens!"

Gently, Bimbo put the kitten down on the grass and picked up the next, and the next.

"See, Cathy, he just wants to get a good look and smell them. That's what dogs do."

After that, the kittens and Bimbo were friends.

Ellen cooked offal for the cats every day. It stunk up the kitchen and congealed in the cats' food dishes lined up against the wall in the back yard.

"Ellen, their dishes are dirty again. They'll get sick with all those germs and smelly old food."

Ellen gave me a look, but said nothing.

In any event, the cats didn't seem to like offal. They preferred their food fresh! All our cats were hunters. They brought birds and mice on to the steps at the front door. They even brought their finds into the house, especially pigeons. Once, they crunched the bones under the dining room table, hidden by the tablecloth hanging down to the floor, while guests sipped beetroot soup and talked politics.

When all the guests were safely outside having coffee on the verandah, William looked under the table to find a pile of blood-covered feathers and a beak.

All our cats had names which we chose with great care and lots of discussion: Soxy, short for Socrates, Fran, Matthew Darlingkins, Fluffy, Emmeline, Jasmine, and Augustus.

Mom let us cuddle up with the cats under the bedclothes when we weren't feeling well and were staying home in bed. The purring seemed to help when we felt rotten. And when we were feeling well, on a winter afternoon, the cats lazed on the window seat in the sitting room to bask in the sun, or curled up on our backs as we lay there dozing or reading.

**

Bimbo was our only dog. He was not a dog who would 'Sit' or 'Lie down' or 'Roll over' on command. And he didn't have official walks. He exercised himself by running round the garden. However, Bimbo wanted to be with us. He most definitely wasn't a watchdog like most of the other dogs we knew. He wasn't an Alsatian. He was an allsorts dog.

Some people trained their dogs, usually vicious Alsations, to attack Africans. Even without training, some dogs would bark and leap up at natives. Many servants and deliverymen were afraid of dogs. But Bimbo was just the opposite. If anyone—regardless of who they were—gave Bimbo a kind word, he would jump up, lick their faces with delight, and stay close beside them.

Bimbo's favourite person was Dad. When Dad paid attention to him, Bimbo would run round and round the lawn in great circles of delight. Bimbo slept on his back, his paws jerking and his legs twitching as he dreamed.

Dick, the next-door-neighbour's Dalmatian, was Bimbo's friend. But William, Eliza, and I hated him. He would come rushing through the gap in the hedge. Whoever he saw first, watch out! He would stand up on his hind legs, with his penis stuck out and start thrusting himself against you. He didn't care if you were a dog or a human.

Before and after Bimbo, we were purely a cat family.

5—FAIRIES

Nobody over the age of about five could be silly enough to believe in Santa Claus, nice as it was to receive presents from him on Christmas Day. Who could really think that a big fat man dressed in red with a big white beard could make his way down each child's chimney to place presents on the mat? And as for flying reindeer? Honestly!

But fairies were an altogether different matter. I knew for sure that they existed, and not just in fairy tales. After all, two people I knew had actually seen them, and one of those people was a grownup.

My friend Janice, who was six years older than me, had fairies in the bottom of her garden. They lived among the tallest flowers, and hid there all day. They only came out at night to dance and sing. She was so lucky. Her garden was very beautiful and large. No wonder the fairies came to live there.

Each time I went to Janice's house, she would tell me more about them, and describe exactly how they looked and what they had been doing the last time she saw them.

Hand in hand, we would rush down to the bottom of the garden. Of course, there were no fairies to be seen. I was there in the day, and they were fast asleep, very well-hidden among the flowers, dreaming the daylight away so they would be ready for dancing as soon as the sun set.

I always hoped that maybe *next* time I would manage to see them— maybe one of them would be waking earlier than usual, or would not have hidden herself so well, and I might see a tiny shoe or the skirt of a gauzy dress in among the petals.

My grandmother Ga had also seen the fairies. She had actually talked to them and could tell me about their conversations, as well as what they were wearing and doing when she saw them.

Every time I had a sleepover at her flat, she would tuck me into the creaky old sofabed in her study—filled with old orange and white or green and white paperback thrillers by Agatha Christie or Ngaio Marsh, and her huge old desk—and sit down on the edge of the bed to tell me the latest news about the fairies. They had specially beautiful voices, high and soft, and they wore frothy dresses, like long ballet tutus, in pale green or blue or pink. They had long hair and wore crowns of flowers.

I could not fathom why the fairies did not seem to want to live at the bottom of my garden. It had many beautiful flowers, and shady places for them to rest, and big lawns for them to dance on at midnight.

But I could never find even one fairy. Perhaps they were frightened of the cats who lived in our house and garden, or perhaps I made too much noise when I went looking for them, and scared them away.

6—FOOD

Ellen was always telling me, "Cathy, you are full of fiemies." That's because I was so pernickety about food. Not only wouldn't I eat soft-boiled eggs with runny yolks—ugh—I wouldn't touch mayonnaise, bread with butter on it—unless it was melty-butter toast—mangoes, or asparagus, artichokes, or, horror of horrors, May's favourite—tongue. And my meat had to be very well done—as in lightly-flavoured charcoal or shoe leather. Any sign of pink and I turned green.

At home, Ellen cooked to suit my *fiemies*, with much teasing and lots of love, always preparing food exactly in the way I wanted it—very well done meat, butterless sandwiches, only scrambled eggs (if I HAD to eat them), and lots of my favourite things.

Ellen was a wonderful cook, and you could also tell her anything that was upsetting you or making you feel very happy. And she was an even better baker than a cook. Nothing beat coming home from school, all grumpy, and finding she had baked her chocolate cake with apricot jam between the layers and chocolate icing for tea, or waking up on a Sunday morning to the smell of scones for breakfast, especially her cheese scones with a little parsley mixed in.

Another weekend treat were Ellen's pancakes, small and thick with lots of melted butter and golden syrup on top. Sometimes she let me help her make them, standing on a chair at the stove, spooning the mixture carefully into the pan, and waiting for the bubbles to pop on the surface and it was time to flip them… and boerewors fried with tomatoes. I wasn't that crazy

23

about Ellen's chocolate squares, but her ginger layer cake, cut into very thin slices, was something to eat very slowly, in tiny bites, so you could enjoy each mouthful. And her ginger biscuits had just the right mixture of crunchy and chewy. Best of all were the hazelnut meringue layers with coffee cream, a special dessert for grown-ups' dinner parties.

We often had asparagus rolls and cheese straws with lots of paprika when my parents invited friends over for drinks. Ellen also made wonderful lamb stew, cider chicken (chicken cooked in cider with lots of lemon), round crunchy chips with well-done lamb chops, roast potatoes with roast chicken for Sunday lunch, well-done roast beef with roast potatoes, gravy, and sweet rolls.

It was always worth visiting the pantry to check the cake and biscuit tins. You might find a treasure—some meringues from last week's dinner party, stale but still well worth eating, or the end of a chocolate cake, the bit with the most icing, or the last ginger biscuit.

I dreaded eating at other people's houses. What if they put a plate of sandwiches with thick butter under the jam in front of me—something that happened almost every time. Sometimes I scraped off the butter or else nibbled miserably round the edges and, shamefacedly, left the rest on my plate. Almost worse than the sandwiches was finding a glass of milk next to my plate, as if I would actually drink that stuff, or if they served the tea with the milk and sugar already in it. Didn't they know I *never* drank tea with milk? My aunt Zoë taught me to drink tea and never had hers with milk. The very smell of milk in tea made my stomach churn. And if it wasn't tea with milk, it was bright orange squash, with not enough water to dilute the sickly sweetness. And what if they gave me the brown meat from the chicken? Did I HAVE to try to eat it?

If I were invited to a friend's house for a swim and *braaivleis*, it might turn into an ordeal, quite apart form the risk of older brothers throwing you into the pool, or the black lab jumping into the pool to try and rescue you. I had to make sure to stand beside my friend's father where he was braaing to make sure he left my piece of boerewors or steak, with all the fat trimmed off, cooking till it was dark brown both inside and out. And if he was braaing *sosaties*, I would have to remove all the chunks of onion and red pepper between the meat, as well as checking if there was any pink left in the lamb, before I could eat. Once I'd made sure of the meat, I had only one more thing to dread: that there would be pawpaw and banana in the fruit salad.

Sometimes at friends' houses, we'd have something completely delicious like their own cook's chocolate cake or biscuits, or fruit salad with lots of granadillas and peaches... but no bananas in it, or pawpaw, or mangoes, and no cream, thank you very much!

**

My grandmother May was a very good baker and cook. But she loved tongue. So when I went to her flat or when she came to our house that is what we had. I hated the thought and the look of it, and the very first time I tasted it, I vowed never to touch it again. The texture and taste were revolting. How could anyone bring themselves to eat an animal's tongue? May also liked to bake cakes with caraway seeds in them. This spoilt the taste. Caraway belonged in rye bread and nowhere else. But I loved May's Mandelbrot, all crunchy with toasted almonds, and her almond tart.

Unlike May, my other grandmother, Ga, did not cook or bake. She had her maid, Florence to do that except at Pesach. Then Ga made the world's best *charoset* because she did not put too much wine with the ground almonds, walnuts, cinnamon, apple, and brown sugar. Other people put too much Pesach wine into their charoset, which completely spoiled the taste. Ga also made *kneidlach* for Pesach and flavoured them with cinnamon and ginger.

For the Friday suppers at Grampa and Ga's flat, Florence made the same meal every time and it was perfect: very well-done lamb chops and steak, boiled rice, potatoes, and tinned peas with, always, a basket of sliced white bread.

"Have some more, Lovey, bread is the staff of life," Grampa would say, offering the basket to me and William. Dessert was ice cream and tinned peaches. We drank red or plain fizzy lemonade from tall and narrow tinted glasses. I liked the bright blue and William had the red glass.

Apart from real, homemade food at meals and teatime, there were wonderful sweets to eat whenever you could. Ga was the great provider of these. Ga always brought sweets in her bag when she came to our house. When she opened her bag, you never knew if she would take out Aeros, Peppermint Crisps, Flakeys, Cadbury's Nuts and Raisins chocolate bars, or Sugus (which had pictures of people in costumes from different countries around the world). Maybe there'd be a box of Smarties. I especially liked the red ones, which I moistened so I could paint my lips with them—they were ALL my favourites. And sometimes Mom or Dad would buy us Top Ten Mint Crisps, the world's best ice cream bar (briefly superseded by the blueback, licorice-flavoured, Count Dracula bars). The only thing better than eating one of those was going to the Milky Lane for a Double Thick Malted Milkshake made with chocolate ice cream, with a marshmallow on top—but the marshmallow had to be very stale for it to be perfect. And there was another kind of ice cream I loved: Italian gelato, the coffee flavour, from Papagallo's in Orange Grove. We only went there as a birthday treat or at half-term, if May was fetching me from school.

For picnics, I loved cold chicken—only the white meat, no skin—cold boerewors (no hardboiled eggs, thank you very much!), chips from a packet, (the chicken or barbecue flavoured), red fizzy lemonade or orange juice, peaches, *naartjies*, and lots of chocolate and chocolate biscuits—plus maybe dried apricots or peaches, or apricot or guava *mebos* to eat in the car on the way there.

For birthday parties, Ellen made treats that were better than any you could possibly find at other people's parties. Besides the birthday chocolate cake layered with apricot jam and lots of icing on top and hundreds and thousands for decoration, we had cookies with icing of different colours, from pink to chocolate to bright blue or bright green or yellow, in their paper cups, and bowls of chips, Smarties, jelly beans, and Licorice All Sorts.

We drank fizzy lemonade and blew those shiny things that unroll and have a feather at the end, and had paper hats and trinkets from crackers that we pulled (with heads turned away for safety). The crackers had the same things inside them as the Lucky Packets at the Zoo—rings with coloured glass jewels, whistles, cellophane fish, or necklaces made out of hard sweets. At the end of the party, each child took home in their lucky bag—a white cake box—some sweets, a slice of cake, and a cookie or two.

7—PRESENTS

In my family, the choosing, giving, and receiving of presents were very important matters. We weren't allowed to make a wish list, but heavy hints were given and, sometimes, acted upon by parents, grandparents, and friends, about what we longed for on our birthdays or for Christmas.

An especially great deal of thought went into the presents we gave to our parents. Sometimes, these were handmade. One year, I made my mother a pincushion out of a pinecone. I painted the pinecone silver. Between the fronds, I put tiny, brightly-coloured pincushions. Mom loved it, and it lived on the glass top of the low cupboard in the dressing room outside her bathroom window for years.

When I was 14 and at high school at Roedean in Uppers, my art teacher was Miss Elaine Marriott. Miss Marriott had white hair and pale blue eyes and hands that were always moving, tracing vague shapes in the air.

The art room was an attic in the Junior School, where Miss Marriott would set up elaborate arrangements of vases, flowers, books, and cloths. She'd ask us to draw them or to draw a cat or a fox. She would be smiling, until she looked at my work. "Cathy, cats don't *have* eyelashes!"

"That vase is blue, not purple. And grass is green, not orange. What's the matter with you?"

But it was Miss Marriott who helped me to make something that became a family treasure—a pottery jug, turquoise on the outside with a pattern incised on it, and white glaze inside. I gave it to my mother for her birthday as soon as the jug had cooled down from the kiln.

Sometimes, Dad, William and I, and then Eliza and Matthew when they were old enough, got together to scheme about a present for Mom's birthday or for their wedding anniversary.

Dad came into the playroom with a big smile on his face, holding something behind his back. "Who wants to help me wrap this present for Mom?"

"Me, me, me!"

He held out a small square green velvet box. Inside was a gold ring set with a huge, pale purple baroque pearl. "OK. Let's find some wrapping paper for it."

This was our cue to dash off to get an empty tissue box, some coloured pages from last Sunday's comic strips from the *Sunday Times,* tissue paper, a shoebox, and lots of sticky tape.

Dad carefully wrapped some tissue paper around the velvet box. Then he put the box inside the tissue box. Then he put the tissue box inside the shoebox. Then he wrapped the shoebox in the comic strips, which William and I stuck down with sticky tape. Finally, we all signed the card that we stuck to the top of the lumpy parcel.

On the birthday morning, we ran into Mom and Dad's room. Dad fetched the parcel from its hiding place in his cupboard and gave it to Mom, who was sitting up in bed in her lacey nightie.

"Ugh, what is this?" she said. "Are you just giving me some old newspaper for my birthday?" She looked very disappointed and scowled at Dad. We laughed and laughed.

She got crosser and crosser as she unwrapped the layers of paper, opening one box after another. When she came at last to the velvet box, she looked very surprised. And when she opened it, she smiled and smiled.

"I thought this time you were really giving me just a box of old tissues. This ring is lovely."

Then she hugged Dad and each of us in turn, and the birthday tea drinking and the birthday chocolate eating could proceed.

At Auckland Park, we young ladies were expected to be able to sew by hand, and so we made dressing-gowns and aprons. My dressing-gown was of pink gingham. Gingham was easy to work with as the checks meant I could sew in straight lines quite easily by following the pattern of the material.

The sewing I was proudest of were the pyjama bags I made for my twin cousins, Sally and Candy. One was of pink gingham checks and the other of blue. I did all the stitching by hand. I took great trouble over the bags, making tiny, even stitches and embroidering their names in chain stitch and even some daisies on each bag. When they were finished, my mother wrapped them up and posted them to Canada, to Toronto, where Sally and Candy had moved with their parents. I liked picturing Sally and Candy putting flowery pyjamas or nighties into my bags, and tucking the bags under their pillows in the morning before they went to school.

**

It was the morning of my fifth birthday. I woke up very early, and crept into Mom and Dad's bedroom, hoping they would be awake enough to give me my first present.

"Go away," Dad groaned, squinting at the clock beside the bed. "It's only five o'clock. I'm still asleep."

But Mom said, sleepily, "Darling, it's too early to climb into bed with us, but you can go on a treasure hunt to find your present. Here is a clue: look in the dining room and the sitting room."

I rushed out of their room and into the dining room. But all I could find were the things that were always there—the round table and its spiky chairs, and the desk that Mom and Dad shared. My face fell. I ran into the sitting room, and there, nestling in the fork of a three-legged tray table, was a huge package. I ripped open the paper and inside was a beautiful dog, white and black, with red lining in his ears. I loved him at once, and for many years after. He nestled beside me while I listened to bedtime stories and cuddled me all night long, as I slept and dreamed.

**

Some of the very best presents came from 'overseas'. Whenever Mom or Dad returned from a trip overseas—one year they met the King and Queen of Greece at a conference for lawyers in Athens, and I saw the photograph of my parents shaking hands with a real king and queen—they brought us wonderful and surprising presents.

As soon as Joseph had carried Mom and Dad's suitcases up the stairs and into their bedroom, William, Eliza, Matthew, and I became very excited. We could scarcely breathe.

Dad made a great show of fumbling with the lock to his suitcase and opening the zipper very slowly.

"Hurry up, Dad." We groaned.

"This case is just full of my old smelly socks and some dirty shirts for Ellen to wash. Why are you in such a hurry to see them?"

At last the suitcase lay open, with its red shiny satin lid resting against the floor. Wrapped packages, large and small, emerged from their hiding places among the neatly-folded clothes and the shoes in their special shoe bags. A necklace, books, soft toys, dolls, a leather belt with a brass buckle in the shape of a giant safety pin, and a long beige sleeveless waistcoat to go with it, the last word in fashion from London. Mom and Dad took turns handing them out.

"Eliza, this one's for you."

"Cathy, this one's for you. I expect it's just a bar of soap from one of the fancy hotels we stayed at."

Inside the beautifully wrapped package, I found a tiny ring with a blue stone.

When I was six, my father came back from overseas bringing me a blue rabbit with very long ears lined in pink cloth. For years, I could not fall asleep without it or without Kosi Bear, the koala bear stuffed toy that the Ovedoff family sent from Australia, from the city with my father's name of Sydney. Blue Rabbit and Kosi Bear slept, one on either side of me, in the top bunk at Number 2.

And then, from his next trip overseas, Dad brought me a cloth doll, an old-fashioned girl in a white lacy dress, with a blue sash, a straw hat, white boots, and a wooden hoop. She had the prettiest, sweetest face I had ever seen on a doll. I named her Emma. Emma came with another doll, also named Emma, a Peggy Nisbet Portrait Doll of Emma Lady Hamilton, in a pale turquoise chiffon dress and red velvet hat.

After that, whenever my father came home from England, he brought me another Peggy Nisbet doll. And when Eliza was old enough to want whatever her big sister had, he brought Peggy Nisbet dolls for Eliza, but different characters, so she had a fine collection as well.

When my collection grew to about 10 dolls, my parents had some special shelves made. They were white, with cupboards and bookcases below and a glass display case on top.

When I was nine, the Barbie doll craze flew across the oceans from America and hit South Africa. Barbie and Ken dolls (her boyfriend with the yellow crewcut) were all I and my friends could talk about, think about, play with, or desire. Every time I visited my parents in chambers, I gazed longingly at the Barbies displayed in Lilliputs, the fancy toyshop on the ground floor of Innes Chambers. I counted the days till my birthday, praying that my parents would give me a Barbie doll of my own so I wouldn't have to rely on visits to my American friend, Nancy, to play with her Barbies.

At last my birthday arrived. It was half term, as well, so school finished early. My parents fetched me from school at lunch time, and brought William and Eliza and Matthew, too, and the family set off to have a picnic beside the Vaal River Dam. We had to drive for miles and miles to get there. I could hardly wait till it would be time to open the presents. I was hoping and hoping that my parents would have realized how much I wanted a Barbie doll for my birthday and would have gone to Lilliputs on their way home one day to buy me a Barbie with beautiful long blond hair that you could comb.

As soon as we sat down to begin the picnic, Dad handed me a package, and I just knew what it had to be, I could tell by the shape of the package, long, narrow and rectangular. I tore off the paper and opened the box... I couldn't believe what I saw. It was not Barbie at all.

"But that's Midge. I wanted Barbie." I burst into tears. Midge had short, dark, curly uncombable hair in a bubble cut. I couldn't even try to sound pleased. Didn't they know the difference between Barbie and Midge?

Mom and Dad exchanged a look.

"*Que c'est que c'est?*" they said, raising their eyebrows.

The wrong doll made even the chocolate cake that Ellen had baked specially, with the apricot jam in the middle and the hundreds and thousands on top, taste wrong.

Later, when we got home and I was gloating and groaning over my birthday loot in the playroom, William tried to cheer me up.

"Let's look through the catalogue. You can choose whatever outfit you want for Midge and I'll buy it for you. With my pocket money, I could probably get you at least two."

We looked through the little book with its pictures of all kinds of outfits and accessories for Barbie. We thought each outfit only cost about five cents, so William reckoned he could well afford to buy me the Barbie outfit with the red swing coat and pillbox hat, or the Friday Date one with the checked dress, white apron, and the tray of sundaes. I felt a little better about Midge, less likely to throw her away and pretend that I had lost her.

But I never really liked her.

Grampa liked to give watches, books, or jewellery as presents. The trouble with the watches was that I lost them or broke them or they just wouldn't work on my wrist. Grampa said perhaps it was because of the static electricity in my body. I had more luck with the jewellery.

Once, on a Jewish High Holiday, Ga and Grampa gave me a Mogen Dovid. I didn't really like the design, but wore it to synagogue once or twice a year on High Holidays. I much preferred the pendant of an uneven polished chunk of malachite in a silver setting, which they brought back from their first trip to Israel. On their next visit, they returned with a small silver ring set with a white pearl. When I was a teenager, Grampa gave me a very grownup royal blue enamel brooch edged with gold, in the shape of a leaf.

One year on my birthday May gave me a most unexpected and beautiful present, a treasure, in fact. On birthdays, and on many unbirthdays as well, May usually gave us all clothes she had sewn or knitted. This time she gave me her silver calling card case, engraved with the initials M.S. The M.S. stood for May Shafner, her maiden name. I kept the Mogen Dovid from Ga and Grampa in the card case.

Sometimes, parcels containing presents would arrive from overseas, from Canada, from my aunts Zoë and Helaine, or from Mom's friend Beryl. These usually came around birthdays or Christmas.

The first hint that there was an overseas parcel came with a delivery note on a card, telling us to come to the post office to pick something up. I nagged Mom till she drove me to the post office.

The clerk handed over a slightly battered, brown-paper-wrapped object.

As soon as we got home, I tore open the brown paper. Underneath there was proper brightly-coloured present-wrapping paper. Inside were several small packages, each neatly labelled in my Aunt Zoë's tiny handwriting. The one for 'Cathy' contained a tent dress made out of paper, with underpants to match. I put it on and paraded around the house. I felt very 'with it' in the dress, sure that nobody else at school would have anything like it.

All day I was very careful not to spill anything, for fear the dress would wrinkle up and disappear into a scrumpled ball like a piece of soggy newspaper.

The package labelled 'Eliza' contained a set of smaller packages of cake and biscuit mixes. All you had to do was add water, stir, and then bake the results in an oven.

William's package held a small carved wooden bear. Matthew's was a stuffed moose to cuddle at night.

Mom's friend Beryl, another South African who had moved to Canada, sent a parcel with nighties for me and Eliza and pyjamas for William and Matthew. Mine was short-sleeved and of soft cotton, patterned with brightly-coloured flowers and insects and the words 'Fresh as a daisy' and 'Cute as a button' repeated over and over.

One of the best overseas presents ever was the one Ga brought me when I was about 12 and she returned from a visit to Canada. Out of her suitcase she took a pair of white bellbottoms with red and blue dots, and a huge flounce for the bell. As soon as I put them on, I knew my friends would all be wild with envy, even though the bell-bottom fad hadn't hit South Africa yet. I would lead the way.

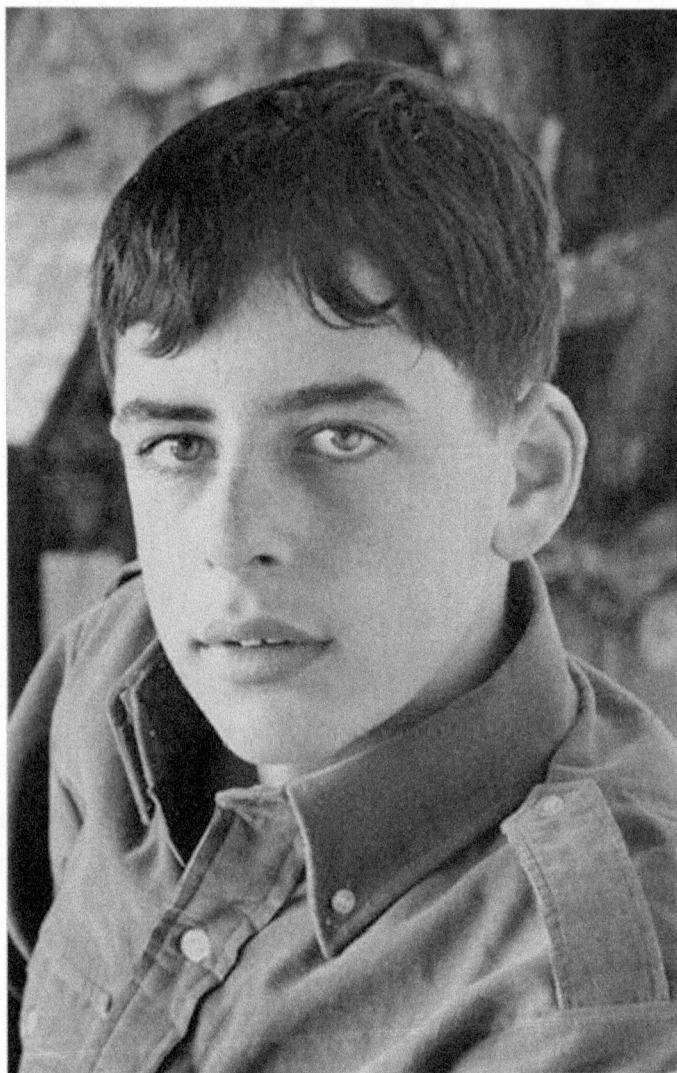

WILLIAM, AT ABOUT 11

8—BIRTHDAYS

On birthdays, besides the presents, certain things always happened in our family. And it didn't matter if it was my birthday or William's or Eliza's or Matthew's or Mom's or Dad's.

It started with a special birthday tea in the morning, in Mom and Dad's room.

As soon as we woke up, we went in to their room. They almost never said "It's too early, go away!"

If I got there first, I went to the white cupboard in their dressing room where they kept the special birthday teaset they'd been given for their wedding. It had two cups and saucers, a teapot, a sugar bowl, and a tiny jug for milk. The pattern was pink and grey flowers on a white background. Then I filled the kettle and plugged it in. It hissed as it worked itself up to boiling point on the dressing room floor. Next, Dad brought out the birthday chocolate from its secret hiding place (which we could never discover). It was always a large bar of Toblerone. We'd have chocolate biscuits, as well. Birthdays were the only times you could eat chocolate of any kind before breakfast.

After tea and biscuits, and chocolate, the birthday person could open one or two presents before going to school.

School on your birthday was not so bad, either. Ellen baked and iced cookies to give to everyone in the class plus a few extra for the teacher—or so I could have more than one—because aren't birthday girls entitled to special treatment?

The birthday day got better and better. Mom came to fetch me from school, and Dad came home early from chambers. Ga and Grampa and May and Morris arrived with presents. We all sat down to afternoon tea in the living room or on chairs on the lawn.

Ellen baked her chocolate cake, with chocolate icing and apricot jam in between the layers. I made a wish as I cut the first slice, as quietly as I could so no one would hear the knife and my wish would come true. The only bad part of a birthday day was when everyone sang *Happy Birthday*, and I cried because I hated that song. Having people sing that song to me was worse than not getting something I had set my heart on, or having the teacher shout at me on my special day, or because my mother forgot to bring the cookies to hand round to the girls in my class, or we had a math or science test and that seemed very unfair on my birthday... The tears were because everyone gathered round the tea table to sing *Happy Birthday*.

"Please DON'T," I begged. But, every year, somebody sang it and made me cry. "The tune is so sad," I wailed, as my father put his arms around me.

Birthdays ended with a special dinner of my favourite foods: lamb chops with Ellen's finely sliced round chips, the hazelnut meringues with coffee cream for pudding, and granadilla juice to drink with dinner, served on the best china.

9—SONGS

But *Happy Birthday* wasn't the worst of the crying songs.

One day, my father put on a record of spirituals and I heard *Way down upon the Swanee River*, sung by a man with a deep, sad voice that seemed to hold all the sorrow of the world in it.

"Why is he so far away from the old folks at home? Why can't he be with his family?" I wept, listening to the longing and sadness in the voice.

As for *Clementine*, this was the saddest song of all. My father couldn't understand why it made me so sad. "It's funny, Darling. Imagine a girl having size nine feet and wearing herring boxes instead of shoes?" He would try to laugh me out of my tears.

"But, Daddy, the miner's darling daughter is lost and gone forever. I can't bear it."

I didn't get any tougher as I grew older. When I was a teenager, I loved folk songs and folksingers. My two favourite singers were Joan Baez and Joni Mitchell. For my sixteenth birthday, I was given a guitar with a beautiful, resonant voice, and sang Joan Baez and Joni Mitchell songs over and over, till they sounded to me like the real thing.

"Cathy, for goodness' sake, stop breaking and splitting your voice like that from high to low, you'll ruin it," said my mother.

The Joan Baez songs were always so sad and desperate, and told of death, love-longing, murder, and despair. I could not sing them without crying. And I cried when I listened, as well. *Barbara Allen* was the worst for tears— "Sweet William died for love of me and I shall die tomorrow."

But lots of the music I heard at our house made me happy. There was always something playing on the gramophone. My parents liked all sorts of music from grand opera to Harry Belafonte, Miriam Makeba, and Ella Fitzgerald. I liked opera, too, and Ella singing songs from the Cole Porter Songbook, such as *You're the Top* or *Fascinating Rhythm* or *Delovely*. First Mom and Dad would dance to the songs, then Dad would dance with me, and Mom with William. My parents were very good dancers.

Sometimes we would listen to Miriam Makeba's world famous *Click Song*. My clicks were not bad, considering I had never been taught how to make those Xhosa sounds. The record album cover photograph showed Miriam Makeba looking extremely elegant in a long silk turquoise-striped dress that fitted very snugly, her hair wound up in a turban of matching colours. Dad and I loved to sing Harry Belafonte's versions of *Jamaican Farewell* as a duet and *Tally me Banana*, which I thought was a funny way of saying 'Carry my bananas.'

Then there was Brendan O' Dowda. He sang Percy French's Irish songs in the most beautiful and melodious baritone: "Oh Mary this London's a wonderful sight, with the people all working by day and by night. They don't plant potatoes, nor cotton nor wheat, but they're all of them digging for gold in the street. At least when I asked them that's what I was told, so I just took a hand in that digging for gold. But for all that I found there I might as well be where the Mountains of Mourne sweep down to the sea."

"Mary quite contrary, come in and shut the door…. Oh, she's listenin' for the whistlin', she's waitin' by the shore for his arums to be warrum round her waist once more!"

Dad and I would sing them together at the tops of our voices. And I could sing 'sharmee shellay' from *Carmen Jones*: "Stand up and fight until you hear the bell. Stand toe to toe, trade blow for blow."

Grampa sometimes bought records of popular numbers from operas or musicals. From *The King and I*, I learnt to love, "Whenever I feel afraid, I whistle a happy tune, the happiness in the tune convinces me that I'm not afraid." That song came in very useful for singing under my breath just before exams, or if I was by myself and had to walk past a scary deserted place.

I couldn't decide whether I wanted to be a Maria Callas and sing grand opera, or an Ella Fitzgerald, only white and with a very high voice, or a Joan Baez and sing heartbreaking folksongs when I grew up. But as soon as I turned 16 and heard the album, *Ladies of the Canyon*, I knew that the only thing I wanted to be was a Joni Mitchell.

10—SEASIDE HOLIDAYS

Holidays, when William and I were small, meant summer holidays. And summer holidays meant the seaside at Plettenberg Bay, on the Cape coast.

Mom and Dad would pack William, Ellen, and me into the back seat of the car, with snacks, blankets, and a suitcase or two at Ellen's feet to serve as a bed when we got sleepy. Then the long long journey to the Cape would begin. There would be frequent stops to go to the lav, or to buy treats, such as ostrich biltong, Top Ten ice cream bars on a stick, Coke, or Fanta.

But the journey was not all wonderful. I often got carsick.

"Dad, stop the car, I'm going to be sick!"

The car would grind to a sudden halt, while Ellen wound down the window, just in time for me to vomit onto the side of the road.

It was a very long way from Johannesburg to the seaside, so we would stay overnight at small hotels in small towns in the middle of nowhere. The roads swirled with red dust and the views from the windows of the ramshackle hotels were of stark Orange Free State or Karoo landscapes. The hotels all served the same breakfasts: Rice Krispies or porridge, fruit juice from a can or bottle, never freshly-squeezed, and canned fruit cocktail.

We would drive and drive for what seemed like forever.

"Are we nearly there?"

"Not for another five hours, Darling."

"But, Mom, we're *never* going to get there. It's taking too long."

"Let's play I Spy," said Dad. "I spy with my little eye something beginning with F."

"Flowers!"

"Fig Trees."

"Fanta!"

At long last, Mom or Dad would announce, "We're nearly there. Who's going to be first to see the sea?"

The Indian Ocean, sparkling below, usually appeared as we crested the top of a hill.

"I see the sea!" William and I yelled out together.

The excitement of "what will the house be like this year?" was an annual event. Would it have a good view of the sea, and, more importantly, be in walking distance of the beach? The rented houses usually came fully equipped with bedding, plates, utensils, pots and pans—and a Cape coloured cook and maid.

William and I gazed at our cook in amazement.

"Did you see that gap in her front teeth?" I whispered to him behind my hand.

"Yes. And what did she say to us?"

The strange woman's singsong voice was heavy with Afrikaans in her English, a completely different sound from the voices of our servants in Johannesburg.

Depending on the size of the house, William and I shared a bedroom or had one each. Ellen lived in the servants' quarters in the back during the holidays.

As soon as we could, we rushed down to the beach with Ellen. Ellen, like the other African and coloured nannies, could wade into the water, perhaps up to her knees. But no one who wasn't white was allowed to swim at the same part of the beach as we did. Their area was miles down the beach, without any kind of lifeguard, the part of the beach the white people didn't even want to go to. And, of course, they could only go swimming when they were 'off'.

Ellen brought bottles of seawater back with her to Johannesburg. On the rare times when she didn't come on holiday with us, I had to promise to bring her back a large bottle of seawater.

"It is very good medicine and very good for your health," she said.

I didn't know how she could bear the salty taste.

One of the best things about going to the seaside was the picnic lunch. First thing in the morning, Ellen, Mom, and Dad would load up the car with towels, suntan lotion, sunglasses, sunhats, sandals, buckets, spades, an umbrella, books for the grownups, and a cold bag filled with scotch ice, cold fruit juice, and fizzy drinks, and maybe a flask of tea or coffee. We also took a basket filled with plates, forks, cups, sandwiches, biscuits, fruit, and chocolate. The sandwiches got very sandy. But there was something about eating them on the beach in the blazing sun, or in the shade of a large beach umbrella, that made them taste so much better than the same sandwiches gone soggy in your lunchbox at school.

At Plettenberg Bay, there was a perfect beach for whatever you wanted to do. The Beacon Isle Beach was best for swimming, whether in the breakers or the lagoon, and for building sandcastles. The Lookout was good for bathing and even better for finding pansy shells and anemones if you walked along the edge of the water in the early morning at low tide. Robberg Beach was best for taking very long walks along firm golden sand, and for doing *pirouettes* and *grand jetés*. The BI beach had a little café where you could buy ice-cream, and flipflops and chips, and candy floss. William and I would beg Mom or Dad to give us each 20 cents so we could go, all on our own, to the Why Not Café to buy something. We didn't mind, too much, the way the owners spoke to us:

"Well, what do you want? Make up your mind. I haven't got all day. There are people waiting." And they never gave us change.

There were usually lots of children to play with, friends from Johannesburg or others we met from day to day. We'd build sandcastles, or go body-surfing in the shallow waves, or look for shells, or join them at their family picnics.

The grownups, especially the women, seemed to think they were still in Johannesburg. They put on their best bikinis and as much of their gold jewellery as they could fit onto their arms and fingers and ears and around their necks. They lay frying in suntan oil in the sun, smoking and gossiping, but never going into the sea. Perhaps they were afraid they'd lose a diamond earring or a heavy gold chain? The sun glittered on their darkening skin and sparkled off their jewellery.

Early in the morning, or later in the day after most people had gone home to supper, people with contraptions for detecting metal beneath the sand would come out. I was sure these prospectors found all kinds of gold treasures that the glittering women had lost.

Plettenberg Bay had a small library that we liked to go to. It was full of books about girls at boarding school in England, where they were all 'chums' and had midnight feasts, stuffing the food down quickly so matron wouldn't find out, and they had names like 'Angela' and 'Daphne' and 'Eleanor'.

We didn't have much to do in the evenings or on rainy days, except read, play Monopoly with each other, or visit friends, or, if we were very lucky, have Dad read to us just before supper or bedtime.

Sometimes, we'd go on outings to the nearby town of Knysna or to the Tsitsikama Forest, where we had to watch out for elephants—though I never saw one there. On the way back, we'd stop at a roadside stall to buy boxes of peaches and lychees.

Some of the houses we stayed in had sand fleas. They made life miserable, with their itchy bites, and we tried all sorts of ways to get rid of them. The one that worked best was our system of shallow bowls and dishes of water to drown them; but more always came in on the clothes, towels, and bags carried to and from the beach.

When I was a teenager, I stopped liking to go to Plettenberg Bay or any seaside holiday place. It always seemed to be that time of the month when we were on holiday. I couldn't swim for several days and had to fend off awkward questions from well-meaning, bumbling friends of my parents: "It's a lovely day, Cathy, why aren't you swimming? Want me to throw you into the water, or get one of those handsome lifeguards to do it instead?"

I would try to laugh, stammering, "I just don't feel like swimming today. Perhaps tomorrow?"

Much worse was not being part of the teen colony. How I *wished* I were, instead of sitting around with my parents and feeling like a spaz. With my sunglasses firmly in place, I gazed over to where the other teenagers were spread out on their towels, the girls flaunting their bikinis and long hair, the boys in their board shorts laughing and showing off, while spreading sand or suntan lotion on the girls—even kissing them! I wasn't brave enough to go over and introduce myself. What if they laughed at me or were unfriendly?

"Can't we leave now? I've had enough of the beach. I want to go home and shower and read my book."

One year, though, on New Year's Eve, I almost got my wish. Richard, the handsomest boy in the teen colony, pinned me down in the sand and kissed me. Then he ignored me for the rest of the holidays.

11—OVERSEAS HOLIDAYS

I was seven and William was five when we went on our first trip overseas. Before and after, there were many times when Mom and Dad went overseas, and William, Eliza, Matthew, and I stayed home. Mom and Dad would hire a Serviceable Sister, such as Mrs. Pike—who drove the Pikey-Likey car—to look after us. William chose the name for Mrs. Pike's small yellow car the moment he saw it.

Mrs. Pike moved into the house and we waited nervously to see what she would be like. Would she be very strict about bedtimes? Would she be kind? Of course, Ga and Grampa and May and Morris came over often to take us out for treats and to make sure we were OK.

We wrote letters to Mom and Dad on thin blue airmail paper and

CATHY, MOM AND WILLIAM IN A HORSEDRAWN CAB IN ROME

received letters from them with foreign stamps. Then they came home with wonderful presents—clothes and dolls for Eliza and me, games for William, and soft toys for Matthew.

But this time, William and I were going overseas, too. Friends of Mom and Dad came to the house, bringing us little gifts to take with us on our travels—a toilet bag, some soap in a tube for washing your clothes in hotel rooms, a diary. The airlines gave each passenger a small navy blue overnight bag, which William and I at once crammed with snacks and books and toys for the long journey.

The flight to England took about 14 or 15 hours, with two stops. The first was at Salisbury in Rhodesia, the second a middle-of-the-night stop in Nairobi, with the temperature a horribly humid 34°C, no ice, and the lavatories blocked. I had a shock in the airport. When I went to the lavatory with my mother, I found black women using the same facilities—not cleaning them, but actually using them! Home was a place where notices said 'whites only' above public lavatories, on park benches, on buses, at beaches, and by the doors to post-offices, banks, and liquor stores. Yet, here was a black woman actually going to use the same lavatory as me and my mother.

I turned to my mother. "Mom, there is an African using our lavatory."

She hushed me and whispered that the rest of the world was different from South Africa. "You can do things there you can't do in South Africa."

In England, we stayed with our Uncle Arnold and Aunt Marian and our cousin Robert, who lived in Watford in a wonderful house called The Grove. The Grove belonged to British Rail, for whom Arnold worked. Ingrid, the German au-pair, looked after Robert. One day as we were having tea and cakes, I complained loudly when Ingrid poured milk into my cup.

"Ugh! Don't you know I only drink black tea? Now, I can't drink it."

She glared at me. "You children don't know how lucky you are! In Germany during the war, we had to put the skin from the top of the milk on our bread instead of butter."

I was afraid she wouldn't like me any more. Yet the next morning, she took William and me to a nearby field where we saw a calf being born, with its long, bloody umbilical cord, and its wobbly legs.

"I think I'm going to be sick," I said, although I couldn't turn my eyes away.

***

Italy was the high point of the holiday. Mom and Dad took us to Rome. They hired a driver and a horse-drawn carriage and we drove all over the city. Mom and I wore headscarves tied under our chins to keep our hair from blowing into our eyes. The carriage stopped so we could get out and climb up the Spanish Steps. Then we drove to the Fontana di Trevi and threw coins into it to make sure we would return to Rome one day; and we ate pizza, pasta, and gelato. Mom bought me a pair of soft golden calfskin shoes, which made me feel like the most beautiful girl in the world.

From Rome we went to the seaside, to Levanto, where the South African family and the Watford family shared a house. It was an old place, quite close to the sea, with a gone-to-seed garden, a high wall round it, and wrought-iron gates. A woman did the cooking, except for the time I decided to make my own version of Rice Krispie Squares. I used corn flakes, cocoa, and salt—which I thought was sugar and added to the mixture in liberal amounts, even though William told me it was salt. It was disgusting and we had to throw it all away... And I rode round and round the garden on the back of the cook's son's motorbike, clinging tightly to the cook's son, with my eyes screwed shut.

CATHY IN ROME IN THE BEAUTIFUL GOLDEN LEATHER SHOES

Levanto had bakeries and pasta shops where we could watch the pasta being made. But the best thing of all was the *gelateria*. There you could try peach, apricot, lemon or pistachio ice cream. At the beach, you could ride in pedalos far out into the blue Mediterranean, and then run back across the burning sand to the umbrella. I learned some Italian words and phrases—*un gelato per favore, un grembiule,* and *uno bambino.*

Johannesburg was very boring after I got back and had told my friends and teachers about my holiday and given presents to them and to Ellen, Lydia, and John. I kept begging Mom and Dad to take us overseas again.

"One day," they said, and smiled at each other.

CATHY—AT ABOUT 13

12—DOCTORS AND DENTISTS

There were some good things about being sick enough to have to see a doctor and stay in bed. There was nothing good about having to see the dentist, nothing at all, and don't even mention the orthodontist—that was worst of all.

When you were sick enough to need a doctor, Mom would phone the GP. A few hours later, he would come round to the house. When you saw him appear with his black leather bag and the stethoscope round his neck, you wished you had not let Mom know how sick you were feeling. But now he was here and there was no use saying you suddenly felt absolutely fine.

You had to sit up in bed in your nightie. Then he put the cold stethoscope against your chest and your back and asked you to breathe deeply. Then he felt for any bumps on your neck. That was scary and ticklish at the same time. Then you had to open your mouth and say "Aaah," while he stuck a wooden spatula into your mouth.

He looked up at Mom: "Cathy has a fever," or "Cathy has mumps," or "I'm afraid that Cathy has German measles." Then he would scrawl a prescription and Mom would phone the chemist with it.

An hour or so later, and there was the put-put-put sound of the chemist's delivery man's little van struggling up the drive.

Then the inevitable drama of trying to take the medicine would begin. I simply could not swallow pills. So if the doctor had prescribed an aspirin, it had to be crushed in a spoonful of apricot jam. You would have a tiny taste of it, and just get the jam, then you would have a bigger mouthful and the bitter pill would hit your taste buds. Holding your nose and closing your eyes didn't help.

Sometimes, the medicine was something you had to drink. It was deep pink and came in a large bottle. It pretended to have a strawberry flavour, but you didn't have to taste more than the tiniest drop on your tongue to realize that the medicine was not very heavily disguised by the strawberry flavour…and the dose called for such large spoonfuls and so many of them, and the level of the medicine never seemed to go any lower.

Then you had to have lots of water afterwards to take away the horrible taste, and then maybe some raspberry jelly, not quite set, to soothe you.

Worse than any pills and bitter medicine was the pain and indignity of getting an injection in my bottom late one night, when I had accidentally hugged a very hot hot-water-bottle to my chest and the water had come gushing out of it. My chest was all red and sore, and I was afraid it would stay that way for the rest of my life.

But being sick had some good things about it. Grampa brought me presents when I was sick—usually books to read. When I was reading the Miss Billie books, he went and bought the series for me. He also brought my favourite sweets. The cats kept me company, sometimes on the bed, sometimes under the bedclothes. I read a lot and slept a lot, with the cats purring beside me.

Ellen brought me food on a tray—all sorts of things that she knew I loved. When I needed anything, I just rang the bell. I had runny jelly, and tea, and well-done lamb chops and her round crunchy chips, and some olive-green tinned peas, which I far preferred to fresh. And a freshly-baked biscuit or slice of cake.

Mom and Dad came and sat on the bed for a chat when they came home from work. They felt my forehead and took my temperature.

It was quite nice to miss school, though then there would be a lot of homework to catch up on. It wasn't too bad being sick as long as you got it just right: sick enough to need to stay home and have the doctor visit, but not too sick so that all you wanted to do was curl up in a ball and groan, or sleep, and the doctor had to give you an injection or make you swallow a pill or some disgusting medicine. Maybe chickenpox or measles was the perfect illness to have, once you got over the worst of the itchiness, soothed with pink calamine lotion that stained your nightie and the sheets and pillow cases and eiderdowns. Those diseases were awful at their height, when you had to scratch and scratch and scratch till the scratches bled, and still they itched.

Mumps were horrible: your face and neck looked deformed with swelling; you couldn't swallow anything, as it hurt too much—not even jelly, or ice cream, or chicken-noodle soup. And you just knew your face would never look normal again.

The family doctor who took over when our favourite one went off to Australia really was not normal. I'd heard my parents talking in low voices.

"I'm afraid he is a little bit mad. We should probably find another doctor…"

That made me feel nervous and fearful. I knew that I had to be on my very best behaviour when he visited, and not let on that I thought there was anything wrong with him. So when he came to the house, I watched and listened anxiously for signs of madness. Would I see it in his eyes, or his strange laugh, or would he say something that didn't make any sense or do something crazy?

He sat on the sofa in the living room, staring at me with his mad eyes, blurting out sentences that didn't mean anything, breaking into laughter at something he heard in his head.

I ran out of the room to Ellen, who hugged me.

Mom and Dad soon found another family doctor for us. And this one was not mad, but very kind, and even visited the servants when they were sick.

**

It was the Saturday of Prize Day when I was in Ante-Matric. You never knew what might happen on Prize Day. Sometimes you would be told in advance that you had won a prize and given a book token so you could go out and buy a book that would then be presented to you by the headmistress or the guest of honour. You would have to go up on the stage in front of the whole school and curtsy and shake the hand of whoever was giving you the prize. You were always afraid you would trip.

But some of the prizes would come as a total surprise to the prizewinner. The teachers were always reminding us of this, so that none of us would dream of bunking Prize Day. On the day, you would arrive with your uniform ironed and starched and your hair neatly plaited or in a ponytail with a green or blue ribbon. You lined up by class and your teacher took attendance. Then you were marched into the hall and seated with the other girls in your class, not with your parents.

On the morning of the Prize Day, I had had a verruca cut out of my foot. My foot felt very sore, too sore to put any weight on it. My parents said I could stay home and that they would go to the school without me.

In the middle of the ceremony, without any warning, the headmistress said, "And this year's scholarship goes to Cathy Kentridge." There was applause and then an awkward, puzzled silence. People began to mutter and look all around them. After a few minutes, the headmistress cleared her throat and went on to announce the winner of the prize for science. After the ceremony had ended, Mom and Dad came up to the headmistress and explained why I was not there.

When I returned to school on the Monday, my teachers were angry with me, and did not believe that my foot had been too painful for me to have been able to attend Prize Day. They said maybe I should not even receive the scholarship. Perhaps I should have limped and grimaced and worn a large and very visible bandage on my right foot? The other girls were happy to tell me how embarrassing it had all been.

Dentists were another matter altogether. Our family dentist had a mouth full of crooked yellowish-brown teeth. That was the first point against him. How could a man with such terrible teeth of his own be trusted to fix yours? Then there was the horrible high-pitched sound of the drill. Worst of all was the pain of the injection that was supposed to numb your mouth, so he could do more work with the drill and put in the fillings.

On top of all that, he told lies.

"Just open your mouth very wide. This is only going to feel like the tiniest pinprick."

And then he would stab your mouth with the injection needle.

The night before going to the dentist was as sleepless as the night before a ballet exam, but the pain did not come from the stab of the curlers into your head. It was from imagining the horrors that the next day would bring. When morning arrived, time started playing tricks, first crawling and then rushing, till it really was time to get into the car and be driven to the dentist's office in town.

"But, Mom, my tooth isn't hurting any more. I don't need to go to the dentist."

"Nonsense. You've been complaining for days about the pain and turning white every time you bite on anything hard. That mouth of yours has to be looked at. Just get into the car."

It was no use crying or throwing a tantrum or trying to run away once you got there. And the marmoset monkey who ran around freely in the waiting room could only distract your attention for a short time. Much too soon, the nurse would come out and say your name. You had to go through the door and climb into the dentist's chair, and sit there with your eyes tight shut and your mouth wide open and your knuckles gripping the arms of the chair so hard that you could see the bones through the skin—if you opened your eyes. But opening your eyes was not a good idea, since then you wouldn't be able to help seeing the injection needle coming towards you, or the drill or the sharp thing with which he prodded around inside your mouth, and your tongue kept getting in the way, and the nurse kept trying to calm you down…

If you had behaved during the appointment, and hadn't yelled or cried or bitten the dentist's hand while he worked on your mouth, you got a reward, a small plaster sculpture of Snow White, or Goofy, or one of the Seven Dwarfs. You could choose which one you wanted, and then take it home and paint it with watercolours.

You felt that maybe you shouldn't eat any sweets or chocolates for a month or a year, so you would never have to go to the dentist again.

There was someone else who was allowed to torture your mouth—the orthodontist. He had hairy hands, a pinky ring, and white shoes, When he put his hand into my mouth I felt there was a spider crawling around inside. My mouth felt battered and bruised after every visit. And by the next day, my mouth would have erupted in ulcers.

"You'll have such wonderful teeth when I'm finished. All the boys will want to kiss you!"

"I don't care."

For the two years that I was having orthodontic work done, I was not allowed to eat biltong, or rusks, or spaghetti because they would damage the wires that were wound round and cemented to my teeth. Bits of wire caught on my lips and the inside of my cheeks. No boy would want to kiss you while you had the braces on, that was for sure! Just the sight of your silvery smile would send them running a mile.

In addition to the braces on my upper and lower teeth, I had to wear a mouthtrap. This was a wire contraption you fitted into small metal tubes cemented to your teeth, then around your head at night to keep your teeth in their new improved alignment. I was lucky; I only had to wear this at night. Some of my friends had orthodontists (and parents) who forced them to wear their mouthtraps to school!

Everybody has to go to the dentist sooner or later, and most of my friends had had measles or mumps. But sometimes, the thing that was the matter with you was so embarrassing, you didn't want any doctor to even know about it, let alone take a look at your body and prescribe some form of ointment or medicine for you to take to make the nastiness go away.

When William was about six and I was about eight, we got very bad cases of ringworm. The circles that appeared just beneath the surface of our skin were disgusting.

"You look like you've got a whole lot of dead shongololo skeletons on your arms and legs," said William.

"Sies! You've got more than I have. I bet you've got them on your back as well!"

When the doctor came to the house, he shook his head and said we would have to take lots of medicine, some to drink and some to chew.

It took weeks and weeks before the ugly circles and scabs disappeared.

The most revolting medical disaster that ever happened to us was getting TAPE WORMS. Some of my friends had had them and told me in very vivid detail about how the worms squirmed about inside your body, and made their way through the various organs, eating all your food, before wriggling out of you when you went to the lav.

"Sies! That's disgusting. I don't believe you!"

Then I got tape worms and I knew that what they had told me was true. It took at least 50 huge bitter and chalky pills, three chewed every day, over the course of several weeks, to get rid of the problem.

13—BOOKS

Books mattered. The good ones left an enduring magic, and the bad, scary, or horrifying ones haunted me for years.

Almost all of my favourites were by English authors. I read almost no South African stories as a child. Except for some short stories by Nadime Gordimer, who was a friend of Mom and Dad's, and sat in her study all day writing, and no one was allowed to knock on the door. We had to read the short stories at school. There was usually something unpleasant that happened in them.

There just didn't seem to be South African literature for children. However, there were the most wonderful animal tales retold by Geraldine Elliott in her books called *Where the Leopard Passes*, *The Long Grass Whispers*, *The Singing Chameleon*, and *The Hunter's Cave*. These tales from Africa and the characters of Kamba the Tortoise, Mvu the Hippopotamus, and Njobvu the Elephant filled my imagination.

My favourite books included almost any book by E. Nesbit—*Five Children and It*, *The Railway Children*, *The Story of the Amulet*, *The Phoenix and the Carpet*, and *The Enchanted Castle* with its terrifying 'Ugly Wugglies' who haunted my nightmares.

I devoured the whole series of *Anne of Green Gables*, and *Pat of Silver Bush* and the *Pollyanna* books. I also loved some of the books my brother William read, such as the Hardy Boys series about boy detectives, and the *William* books by Richmal Crompton.

Enid Blyton's *Famous Five* and *Secret Seven* books were a forbidden, guilty pleasure to be enjoyed at the homes of friends, whose parents did not have such high standards for literature as mine.

And then there were the stories by Angela Brazil about girls at a boarding school in England. How I longed to go—until I went to Roedean. There I began to realise what boarding school life was really like—its bitchiness, how nasty the girls could be to each other, how lonely it could be, its petty fights, the power of some of the girls, the house mistresses and the teachers to make one's life miserable, not forgetting the very small number of weekends at home or Sundays out. These could be cancelled for the least infraction of a school rule, or on a whim by a prefect or teacher. Almost worse was the school food, which was beyond awful.

I treasured *The Unhappy Hippopotamus*, with its unforgettable black, pink, and white cover of Harriet Hippopotamus dabbing her eyes with a dainty lace handkerchief, while tears streamed down her face.

My copy of *Jeanne-Marie Counts her Sheep* was almost worn out with rereading. I had tried to write my name on the front page and to fill in some of the illustrations with orange crayon. I felt very proud to be able to say the French names in the book. "Patapon, some day you will have one little lamb. Then we can sell the wool and we'll buy everything we want." Patapon answers, "Yes, I shall have one little lamb. We shall live in the green field where the daisies are white and the sun shines all day long. We shall grow wool for you, Jeanne-Marie."

And *Trovato*, the story of the lost little Italian boy, by Edward Ardizzone, with his beautiful watercolour illustrations.

When I was a lot older, I read *Gulliver's Travels* and then *Mistress Masham's Repose*, which takes up the story of some Lilliputians who escaped from captivity and lived a secret life in the summer house of a huge country estate in England.

My father read to William and me, and then later to Eliza and Matthew, many of the great classics of English literature by Dickens, Jane Austen, and the Bronte's.

From all this reading, I knew and loved and understood the English countryside far better than the South African landscape.

When I was a teenager, I found in the backroom on the high shelves the books that I was *not* supposed to read, such as Simone de Beauvoir's *The Second Sex*. I was attracted by the word 'sex'. It seemed a very dry book—until I came to the description of her seduction.

Then there were the books about The Saint, with lots of sexy bits. I didn't quite know what was happening in the descriptions, but it sounded exciting and forbidden.

There were three Afrikaans books that haunted me in different ways. *Die Aamborstige Klok* was a memoir of life in a small town. You could almost taste the words: "Mrs. Ball's *Blatjang*" and the expression "rara avis." And reading the battered copy of *Sonde met die Bure*, about a family that goes travelling with a pet elephant, was one of the few joys of studying Afrikaans at high school.

But *Die Skarlaken Eskade* was something altogether different. It was about a secret Scarlet Squadron which went about attempting to rescue people, not always successfully, from being plunged into vats of boiling acid. Or perhaps the secret Scarlet Squadron did the plunging. I was never quite clear about that. The teacher seemed to relish the horror of the story. I couldn't understand why such a book had been chosen for the syllabus. Secretly, I and the other girls thought it proved how "nasty" Afrikaners really were.

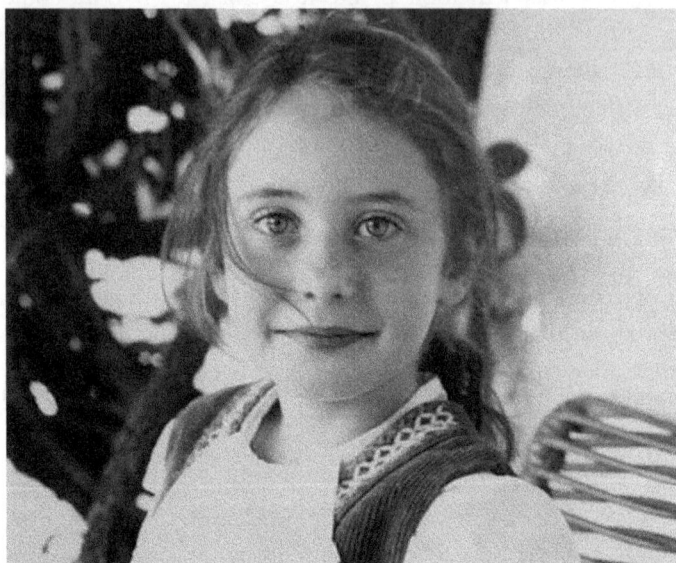

ELIZA—AT ABOUT FIVE

14—POLITICS

Everyone was always talking politics. You couldn't get away from it. Politics meant—

- Going from having Queen Elizabeth as our queen in England to becoming The Republic of South Africa with a President
- Changing from using pounds, shillings, and sixpences to using the decimal system of rands and cents.
- Changing from singing *God save the Queen,* to having to learn a new national anthem, *Die stem* in Afrikaans. Not having any English words for it. Not even knowing exactly what the words meant.
- Getting a new flag—in blue, orange, and white.
- Having to learn more Afrikaans and speak it and hear it more often.
- Having the hated Afrikaners and National Party in power
- The assassination of the Prime Minister Dr. Hendrik Verwoed in Pretoria. A uniformed Parliamentary messenger called Tsafendas had made his way into the very centre of the Parliament Buildings and stabbed Dr. Verwoed in the heart with a knife. I was 10 when the news was announced at school. I didn't know whether to be solemn and sad or to cheer.
- Politics meant "they" and "we."
- *They* were Africans (In our family we were never allowed to call them "natives" or "Bantu" and the use of "kaffir" was a punishable offence).
- Sometimes "they" meant Afrikaners.
- The African *they* lived with different rules and laws from ours. They had to ride on different buses, the stinking green and white Putco buses. They were not allowed to live in white suburbs or white areas of Johannesburg. They had to use separate entrances to the post office and the bank and the liquor store. They had separate public lavatories and

separate lavatories in the houses or businesses where they worked and they had separate benches in the park.

- They were only allowed to do certain jobs and not allowed to do others.
- They walked everywhere in the suburbs. You hardly ever saw a white person walking. We were driven everywhere, by our parents or the chauffeur (who was never white).
- They worked for us and had to live far away from their children. We passed on our cast-off clothes to them, especially at Christmas, when we gave them new clothes as well, for themselves and their children.
- They were not allowed to belong to any political party.
- The Afrikaner "they" spoke what I thought was the ugliest language in the world.
- *They* were always rude and arrogant when they talked to or about or had any dealings with Africans.
- They despised English-speaking South Africans.
- They belonged to the Dutch Reformed Church.
- They had a secret, very powerful society called 'Die Broederbond'.
- They created apartheid.
- They banned books, music, magazines, and people, especially those they didn't like or were afraid of.
- They didn't live in the same suburbs as we did, and the rich ones were in Pretoria and Cape Town.
- You could be a Liberal (like my parents and all their friends) or belong to the United Party or be a Nationalist, (a Nat)—the party that Afrikaners belonged to.
- Politics meant election posters that said "Vote Liberal, if you want a black man living next door!" Or "Be a man not a mouse, vote for Gita Dysenhaus."
- Politics meant that our friends—Dr. Selma Browde and Mrs. Helen Suzman—were two lonely voices for the rights of Africans. Selma Browde was in the Provincial Council in Pretoria, and Helen Suzman was in Parliament in Cape Town.
- Politics meant The Black Sash: White women standing together on street corners, with black sashes over their dresses, to protest at the government's treatment of non-whites.

15—AUCKLAND PARK

It was Miss Jennifer Hallet, head of my nursery school, The Green School, who suggested to my parents that they send me to Auckland Park Preparatory School.

APPS was a 40-minute drive from our house through heavy traffic and there were many good schools a lot closer, but my parents followed her suggestion. This is how it came about that Grampa drove me to school there every day for seven years, going miles and miles out of his way to do so.

It was just past seven in the morning. The kitchen door opened and Grampa walked in.

"*Boker Tov!*"

"*Boker Tov*, Grampa!" William, Ellen, and I answered in unison.

He sat down at the breakfast table where I was just finishing my fruit salad and dreading having to try to swallow the scrambled egg congealing on the plate in front of me.

I lifted the fork to my mouth and sniffed the eggs. Ugh! Ellen and Grampa began their daily ritual of trying to get me to eat them.

"Eat them, Cathy. I made them just the way you like them. Not too runny," said Ellen.

"But I don't want to."

"Eat them, Lovey. They're good for you," said Grampa.

"But I don't like eggs." I made a face. "Besides, I'm not hungry."

"You must eat them, Lovey. You can fool me, but you can't fool your tummy and you can't fool God."

I didn't answer; I was too busy putting up a barrier of cereal boxes around my plate so I wouldn't have to watch William eating his soft fried eggs with runny yolks. Sometimes, William teased me by peering over the cereal boxes with his mouth dripping egg yolk.

"Grampa, tell him to stop. Now he's making me feel sick and I really can't eat my egg."

"Time to go. *Tempus fugit*, time waits for no man," said Grampa, pointing to his gold watch.

So I'd set out for school leaving most of my scrambled eggs on the plate. Then, sure enough, a few minutes later after we had dropped William off at his school, which was much nearer than mine, I would start to feel very hungry.

"Grampa, please can we go to the bakery for an Italian roll?"

And Grampa, who could not refuse his grandchildren anything, drove me to the bakery to buy some of the crusty rolls I loved so much. I ate one in the car and kept the other for school lunch.

**

At Auckland Park, we wore blue and white checked dresses, green blazers, and white Panama hats with a navy and green ribbon. The school crest was a lighthouse.

The headmistress, Mrs. Gilham, was from England and lived with her elderly mother in the house next door to the school. Behind her back, we all called her 'Gilliwigs'.

Another import from England, as Gilliwigs proudly told us, was the house system. As soon as you arrived at the school, you were put into a house—St. Patrick's, St. Andrew's, or St. George's. I was in St. Patrick's, which was the green house. We competed fiercely on Sports Day and at the Swimming Gala, yelling encouragement to our

CATHY IN HER AUCKLAND PARK PREPARATORY SCHOOL UNIFORM.

own team and booing the others. Before every Gala and Sports Day, we spent hours making rosettes out of ribbons in our house colours, wound and stitched around a cardboard circle. If you were in the Swimming Gala—and if you could swim, you *had* to be in it—you wore a plain black one-piece bathing suit and a bathing cap in the house colour. When you were not swimming in the freezing water—the Galas were always held in March, just as the weather was turning chilly—you sat around the pool, grouped in houses, and waved banners with the house name on them.

"Come on St. Patrick's! Come *on*!"

Almost all the children at the school were whites and Anglicans. But there were one or two Chinese children—even though the Chinese weren't counted as white. Japanese children were regarded as "honourary whites." I never found out why.

I was one of a handful of Jewish children at the school.

One day, Mrs. Gilham summoned my friend Sally and me to her office. We had no idea what we had done, but we knew that the headmistress only wanted to see you if you'd done something seriously bad.

"Cathy and Sally, I am very disappointed in you. I hear you've been calling Suzanne names," she said.

We hung our heads, nodding miserably. Suzanne was the Chinese girl in our class. Someone had overheard us saying "Ching Chong Chinaman," and pulling our eyes till they slanted to look Chinese, and had told on us.

"Cathy," said Mrs. Gilham fixing her small blue eyes on me, "how would you like to be called Jew, Jew, Jewess?"

I'd never thought about that. I looked down, muttering, "I'm sorry."

We poked fun at another girl who was different from the rest of us. She had a way of laughing at anything and nothing, and of rubbing her hands together with her mouth wide open.

"Come over here, we've got something for you," we called out to her and she came lolloping over, her mouth hanging open and her hands rubbing together faster than ever. We held up our closed fists, then opened them and said, "We've got nothing for you, that's what we've got!" and laughed when she ran away crying.

There were only three things that I really enjoyed at Auckland Park Preparatory School: the Catch-the-Train Race on Sports Day, the handstand competitions at break every day, and the annual Flower Arranging Competition.

For the Catch-the-Train Race, the track was dotted with piles of clothes and belongings—suitcases, umbrellas, pairs of shoes, and dresses.

"On your marks, get set, go!" yelled the games-teacher, blowing her whistle very loudly.

We dashed off, each picking up first a suitcase, then putting on a dress, then a pair of grown-up high heels that were much too large. As we stumbled along, we had to put a pair of socks into the suitcase (which invariably had a broken lock) and finally open the umbrella, which was guaranteed to turn itself inside out, all in our rush to catch the train.

I won the race once, but I think that was because the girl in the lead tripped over her feet in their high heels and I pulled ahead and crossed the finishing line first.

But there was no doubt as to who was Queen of the Handstands. I reigned supreme. There are photos to prove it—first, the skinny dark-haired girl upright in a ballerina pose, then the same girl upside down with her legs straight and toes pointed in the air. I could keep that pose for great lengths of time and walk with ease on my hands. At the command "Handstands UP!" I was always the first up and the one who stayed straight and unwobbling long after the other girls tottered to the ground.

I did handstands at home in the garden, in the hallway, in the kitchen, in my bedroom. And in the swimming pool at Gladys and George's. They were friends of Mom and Dad's, and we were sometimes taken there for a swim. Phineas, their cook, brought us cold pancakes with thick butter to have with our tea. After a long swim, and eating lots of pancakes, you could climb up to the roof of the change room and bake in the sun to get dry.

The annual Flower Arranging Competition had several categories. The ones I was interested in were Cut Flowers and Wild Flowers. I loved finding things in our garden–wild flowers, leaves, regular flowers, and twigs, and then arranging them dramatically and beautifully. You were allowed to use little mirrors for ponds, and pebbles for rocks, and plastic geese, swans, and ducks. On competition day, I arrived at school with a basketful of flowers, plants, and some bowls and got straight to work. I entered the wildflower category and the cut flower category. I created landscapes with wildflowers and twigs and leaves, with a few pebbles here and there. Then I carefully arranged roses, daisies, anemones, and agapanthus in a tall vase. I was very pleased with my efforts.

But it was no good. Carol won First Prize—again—she of the perfect hair. Her arrangements were sickly sweet. We all thought so. Carol's prize-winning creation used an empty chocolate box filled with white daisies cut off very short and arranged in symmetrical rows around a mirror pond. I was ready to spit nails when she was given First Prize and I received only an Honourable Mention.

I didn't like most of my teachers at APPS, from Mrs. Wilson in Grade One teacher, to my sarcastic last teacher there in Standard Five.

Mrs. Wilson made us line up beside her desk to take turns reading aloud about Janet and John.

"See Janet jump. John jumps too." What could be easier? But the boy in front of me stuttered and stumbled, "S..s..s see JJaa..net jump?" till I was frothing with impatience and I sighed loudly.

"We can't all be as clever as you, Cathy!" snapped Mrs. Wilson.

But being forced to take turns to read aloud was nothing to the horror of compulsory school milk, in small glass bottles, delivered to the school each morning, and left sitting in a crate in the hot classroom. By break, the milk was lukewarm and sour. Mrs. Wilson didn't care. She didn't have to drink it.

"Cathy, you will stand here and drink your milk or you won't be allowed out at break," she said.

I choked as the curdled milk trickled down my throat, while Mrs. Wilson stood glaring down at me.

In Standard One, I learnt exactly two things. One was to hate the name David, because a pale warty boy called David sat behind me and dipped my pigtails in the inkwell.

"Mrs. Weston, David is dipping my hair in the ink, again," I called out.

David smirked.

Mrs. Weston shouted at him and continued with the lesson.

We were learning to write cursive, with pens that you dipped into an inkwell in your desk. That was the only other thing I learned in Standard One. You tried to copy the beautifully-written handwriting sheets which said "Xerxes, King of Persians." But the samplers never told us anything about Xerxes, except that he had far too many x's in his name. However, my pen was forever making blots and splotches on the paper, covering my fingers and clothes with navy-blue ink, so in my report, I never got above a C minus for handwriting skills.

My troubles with David did not end when the bell rang. If my mother was not right there waiting at the gate to fetch me, David ran over to the huge itchyball tree outside the school, picked up a handful of the prickly balls and stuffed them down the back of my dress, while I screamed with rage and pain.

Luckily for us, by Standard Three, the boys were gone to boys-only schools. Luckily for them, they didn't have our Standard Three teacher teaching them. We were all rather afraid of her. She came from England and nothing we ever did seemed to please her.

There was a plumply pretty girl in our class called Jennifer. She had curly brown hair and brown eyes. She had a very pretty English mother, too, with auburn hair, no father present, and lived with her mother and grandparents in the suburb of Blackheath. She had a passion for Cliff Richards and Elvis Presley. The rest of us despised and mocked them, far preferring the Beatles. Jennifer also had a passion for Hayley Mills, the star of *Pollyanna*, a smash-hit film we had all just been to see.

But we all envied anyone whom Jennifer invited to her house. They were sure to get a wonderful afternoon tea of cucumber sandwiches, cake, orange juice, and sweets. And Jennifer would show them her huge collection of toys and records, and clothes.

One day our teacher, Mrs. Bowskill, asked each of us to tell about her hobby.

"Mine is Cliff Richards," said Jennifer. "I have 150 photos of him."

"That must be quite a hobby in itself, just counting the photographs!" said Mrs. Bowskill.

We sniggered.

But suddenly we all felt Mrs. Bowskill might make fun of each of our hobbies and we didn't want to talk about them in front of her.

She did, once, do something fun with us. It was the last day of term and all our exams were written and marked.

"Let's play charades," said Mrs. Bowskill, and explained how the game worked.

My team had to act out *catastrophe*. Mrs. Bowskill whispered to us how to break the word up into different parts and act them out separately as 'Cat-ass-trophy.' Nobody could guess the word for ages.

There were one or two nice, young, pretty teachers at the school. One of them always held one hand tightly clutched into a fist, with a white lace handkerchief dangling from her clenched fingers. I watched and waited for seven years to see if the hand would open. It never did.

And then there was Miss Merlin Carter. All the girls in my class were infatuated with Miss Carter. We were the envy of every other girl in the school, who all longed to be in Standard 4, taught by Miss Carter, who was tall and slim with curly, short strawberry blonde hair. She made lessons so interesting and fun. Best of all, she had a tea-party at the end of the year and invited the whole class to her home, a few minutes' walk from the school.

But when we looked for her at the start of the next year, she was gone.

The art teacher wore bright clothes and huge rings. But the most powerful thing about her was the pungent perfume she wore. It preceded her into the art room and lingered long after she had left. Art classes were fun if you didn't mind the smell.

There were other strong smells at the school.

When you used the lavatories at the school, you had to wash your hands with bright red Lifebuoy soap, which was powerfully smelly and something that none of us would ever use at home. There, we would use sweet-smelling Lux, Pears, or Dove soap. At home, carbolic Lifebuoy soap was the soap that white madams bought for their house and garden 'boys'.

Every schoolchild had to learn Afrikaans and it was an unwritten law that you had to hate it and do as little as you could get away with in class, and learn as little as you possibly could.

Every morning, Mevrou, the Afrikaans teacher, smiled at us. "Girls, sit nicely *bymekaar*. Now sing '*Hoe ry die boere sit sit so, sit sit so, sit sit so, hoe ry die boere sit sit so, sit sit so, hoerrah!*"

Twenty tuneless voices shouted out the words.

The only time you could have fun in Afrikaans was during exams. Mevrou set up suitcases and books on the desks between us so we couldn't cheat or chat. But we usually found a way to at least exchange smiles or groans, though you had to be careful not to be caught, or Mevrou would pounce.

"I'm sending you straight to Mrs. Gilham, and I will give you a big round nought for your exam!"

The time in Standard Five at APPS was both good and bad.

One of the bad things was that puberty hit. One morning, towards the end of my last term there, when I was about 12, Grampa was driving me to school. The sun shone and the windows were rolled down. I was wearing a regulation sleeveless school dress, perfect for a hot summer's day.

I lifted my arm to pat my pigtails to make sure they were still neatly tied with their green ribbon. "Ugh!" There in my armpit were two long black hairs. I quickly looked under the other arm. That armpit had three long black hairs.

I *could not* go to school and risk the other girls seeing that I had hairy underarms.

"Grampa, we have to go home."

"Oh, Lovey, are you not feeling well?"

"I'm all right, Grampa, I'm just so cold, I need my cardigan."

"But, Lovey, it's a hot day. You *must* be feeling sick if you need a cardigan today."

And he turned the car around to take me home so I could pick up the cardigan, button it all the way up, and go to school with no chance of my shameful secret being discovered.

The good thing about being in Standard Five was that it meant you were in the last year of preparatory school. The next year you would start high school somewhere else and never have to see these teachers or this school again.

The Standard Five teacher had a Twiggy haircut (short on one side, long on the other), and wore only one earring, since her hair covered the other ear.

She prepared us for the posh private high schools to which most of us would be going, if we passed the entrance exams. But she did not seem concerned about how much English or geography we knew.

A few days before the exam, we learnt what was really necessary to succeed at a posh high school.

I had just raised my hand to ask for permission to be excused.

"Any girl who hopes to get in to Roedean or Kingsmead should never draw attention to the functioning of her bowels. Cathy, you can just wait till the end of the lesson."

Apparently, in high society, it was considered better to suffer agonies than ask to go to the lavatory.

A few months later, when I had left APPS and was half way through my first year of high school, I itched to tell her what I had learned: no one at Roedean cared how often you asked to go to the lavatory, but if you wanted to fit in and be accepted by the other girls, you had to be able to swear fluently and use 'fuck' at least once in every sentence.

16—CRAZES

We always had some kind of craze going on at Auckland Park Preparatory School. One season it was French knitting, which went on frantically at breaks while the craze was at its height. You needed four nails, a wooden cotton reel, and balls of brightly-coloured wool. You could make wonderful long woollen snakes to arrange in a circle to stitch together into a braided mat to give your mother for a birthday or to put on your bedside table. Fierce rivalry went on as to whose snake was the longest.

And then there were Skoobydoos—plastic strands you wove into intricate patterns to be worn as bracelets or used as key chains. My friend Mary was the best at Skoobydoos and there was no design she couldn't do—square, diagonal, outside braid, inside braid. She made them into key chains, bracelets, and sandal tops. If you were very nice to her and gave her some sweets, she'd help you begin the pattern for a fancy Skoobydoo.

Whenever the skipping craze struck, we would raid our mothers' sewing boxes for long pieces of thin elastic. You tied the ends together in a knot. A girl stood inside each end of the loop, with the elastic around her ankles and her feet wide apart. They moved further and further away from each other till the elastic was tight. The skipper did a series of intricate jumps and twirls, yelling "salt, pepper, mustard, vinegar!" and jumping faster with each word as she leapt in and out of the elastic loop. If you completed one set without tripping, the holding girls moved the elastic a little further up their legs.

You could do this kind of "French Skipping" on your own, or in a team with one or two other girls. One day I went through a faultless series of skips till the elastic was up around their knees. Then I tripped and shinned my knee on the asphalt. I was much better at skipping with a skipping rope, to the same "salt, pepper, mustard, vinegar, vinegar, vinegar!" I could count

CATHY, AT ABOUT 15, IN THE FAMOUS YELLOW AND PURPLE LINEN DRESS WITH THE ZIP IN THE FRONT,

inside my head to 200 without tripping over my feet or running out of breath.

The craze that aroused the strongest feelings was Swops. These were small printed pictures, which you could stick into special albums or carry around in a painted tin to look at and enjoy. We could think of nothing else. Each morning I rushed to school, clutching my tin, full of schemes for enlarging my collection and trading some ordinary Swops for a treasure.

"Sally, I've got lots of flowers. I know you like them. Would you swop that old Cupid for two roses?" I said, trying not to show how much I wanted the Cupid.

"No, you jolly can't have my Cupid. I don't even like flowers anymore. So wah!"

I'd have to try and trick somebody else into parting with a precious Cupid.

We had crazes at high school, too. One year it was "Egyptian sandals." You braided strands of raffia in red, green, blue and gold, and threaded beads onto them to make the upper part of a sandal. A loop went over your big toe and you tied the ends of the braid around your ankle. The beads sparkled on your foot. If you were very creative, like Julia, you worked out how to make raffia flowers for your sandals as well. Each of us had several pairs.

But the biggest and most long-lasting craze at Roedean was boys. How to meet them, who you'd 'got off' with last weekend at Rosemary's party, who you were hoping to get off with this weekend at Laura's party. What to do about that guy that you were crazy about, but who had got off with Jane at the last party. Why did a huge pimple appear on your chin before the party you'd been looking forward to for ages?

And what do you do to attract a boy? What do you wear, what do you say? Should you try to look sexy or only pretty? One day I went to a party in a new yellow and purple dress with a zip up the front. I felt very pretty. Suddenly, a dreadful idea struck me—what if some boy unzipped the dress and I would be exposed in my pink gingham bra? So I put on a white and pink cardigan, buttoned it up to my neck, and was a wallflower all night, unwillingly and enviously overhearing the giggles and smooches of the lucky ones at the party. *(Previous page: Cathy in the famous purple and yellow dress with the zip in the front.)*

As for the poor Roedean boarders, who were barred from any contact with boys during term time, but used all their ingenuity to sneak out at night to rendezvous with boys from the neighbouring all-boys' school... we could only gasp when they told us their exploits next day. These were the same girls who spent their holidays 'getting off ' with every boy they met—if you believed what they said when they got back to school.

I envied every girl who had an older brother, and cursed my parents for having me first and not William. In the pursuit of a boyfriend, what use in the world was a younger brother? Why oh why had my parents chosen to send me to an all-girls school? How would I ever find a boyfriend?

At break, at lunch, and in between classes, we talked and talked about boys; we made jokes with double-meanings and nudged each other to make sure we got it. We dreamed of university, where there would be all kinds of wonderful boys to meet any time we wanted.

**

When I was 17, I had what none of us at Roedean could ever have dreamed of in our wildest imaginings of lust and desire. I went to England to an all-boys school with 20 girls in the Sixth Form and hundreds of boys. A place where I could have the choice of any boy I wanted to be my boyfriend, and could glory in the thought that scores of them would have done anything to 'get off' with me.

17—FAMILY SAYINGS

There was something about these expressions that we couldn't resist. From the first time we heard them, they became part of our family's regular vocabulary.

- "Nice, but only QUITE nice." —from one of William's teachers. Used to express modified rapture about anything or anyone.
- "You Bladdy Ox!" —what I taught my nursery school teachers to call each other.
- "Maar eers…Lav toe!" —from "The Blob," one of William's teachers at King Edward VII School (KES). ("But first I must go to the lav!")
- "Klas, wat het Kentridge gemaak? ("Class, what did Kentridge make?")
  " 'N gemors." ("A mess.")
  "Watter soort gemors?" ("What sort of mess?")
  " 'N blerrie gemors." ("A bloody mess.") Origin: The Blob asking the class what they thought about William's homework.
- " 'N poeverige poging." ("A feeble effort.") The Blob's equivalent of my French teacher's "Six is such a wishy-washy mark."
- "If you don't keep your verbs strictly under control, you will all fail. 'OPPlessly!"—from William's Italian Latin teacher at KES.
- "I don't eat fowl."-—Peggy at lunch in the garden at Number 72 one Sunday.
- "Do you have any loo bumph?" -—Peggy at lunch in the garden on another Sunday.
- "Mommy, why does Peggy have such a SILLY voice?" —Matthew, aged

four, voicing a universal sentiment at lunch in the garden one Sunday.

- "Wanton Extravagance" or "W. E." – to describe the purchase of an expensive item one doesn't really need, but which one could not resist.

- "Six is such a wishy-washy mark – I think I am going to faint!" – My French teacher's invariable response to my most recent French grammar test.

- "You're the oldest, but I'm the sweetest" – William's words, at 5, to me.

- "Shall I go and kick him?" said in response to any time anyone had said or done something to hurt the feelings or physical person of any member of the family. Origin: William, aged three, kicking a hairdresser who was making me cry by pulling too hard on my scalp when trying to untangle the knots in my hair.

- "Mrs. Raikes' Old Vest!"— said in response to ideas about what to wear to a special event. Origin: a game Dad and I played before my first school dance, to laugh me out of my anxiety, not just about who would or could be my escort, but what dress I should wear. We took turns asking each other questions and always got the same answer.
  "What would you like for dinner tonight?"
  "Mrs. Raikes' old vest."
  "What will you wear for your Intermediate ballet exam?"
  "Mrs. Raikes' old vest."

- "But what did HE do?" said to elicit information about any funny occurrence. Origin: an unintentionally hilarious performance of "Three Cheers for Pooh" by an Afrikaans school at a choral speaking competition in which I participated when I was at Auckland Park.

- "I thought YU KNEW!" said in response to a piece of news, not earth-shattering. (Origin as above)

- "DEAR-REST, TELL ALL!" origin — our family friend Helouise's enthusiastic and encouraging response to any information you cared to impart, especially if it might be a juicy piece of gossip. Standard usage when one member of the family was trying to entice another to relay something important or funny to the rest of the family.

- "It's the ULTIMA Thule!" – a Helouise expression of bliss, used by our family to describe anything from food to weather to clothes or a landscape.

- "This year you gave me clothes, last year you gave me clothes, next year

I won't invite you to my party!"—William's response to his friend Michael's choice of birthday present for him.

- "I'm a bit nips!" — example: "I forgot to take the butter out of its package before I put it on the dinner table. I'm a bit nips about what Mom will say."
  Or, "I've got a speech to make tomorrow and I'm a bit nips about how people will like it."

- "Poep scared," a much stronger version of the above. Example: "I'm poep-scared to go to class. Madame will kill me because I left my French book at home." As in "I'm shit scared."

- "There will be NO eggs eaten in this room!" Me at Pine Lake Inn giving orders to a waiter who was bringing in breakfast trays to me and William.

- "Que c'est que c'est?" (pronounced "Kess kuh say?") – what Mom and Dad said to each other when they didn't want us to understand what they were saying.

MATTHEW—AT ABOUT TWO.

18—THINGS WE SAID

- "We walk straight so you better get out the way; we walk straight so you better get out the way." Said when walking along with friends, arms folded.
- Question: "Are you a PLP?"
Answer: "Yes."

  Questioner: "Oh, so you're a Public Leaning Post?" and leans up against the answerer.
Answer: "No."
Questioner: "Oh, so you're not a Proper Living Person?"

- "Lez-be friends" – something we said to each other on Thursdays at Roedean. For some reason, Thursday was Lesbian Day.
- "I laugh (pronounced: 'larf') you fell down climbing on that wall." Meaning "I'd laugh if you fell off doing a stupid thing like walking along that wall."
- "He charfed me his father was a policeman." Meaning "he pretended to me that his father was a policeman."
- "Who did you get off with at Penny's party?" meaning "What guy did you kiss at Penny's party?" The biggest question when conducting a post mortem of any party anyone had been to over the weekend.
- "Afrikaner *vrot* banana" meaning "Afrikaner, rotten banana"—what we whispered to each other when we met an Afrikaner.

- "Johnny's out of jail," said when someone's bra strap or petticoat was showing.
- "I've got the curse," meaning, "I'm having my period."

19—THINGS TO SNEER AT

My friends and I liked to sneer at:

- Radio Bantu with its Bantu music and voices
- Afrikaners
- Any Afrikaans music, because it was always performed on squashboxes
- The Dutch Reformed Church, which we, like many others, called the "Dutch Deformed Church," with its fulminating apartheid-preaching ministers and congregants
- Men who wore their hair very short, with "short back and sides" and wore green- or khaki-coloured safari suits (which had half belts of the same fabric at the back of the short sleeved shirt, and shorts rather than trousers). The people who wore these styles were almost all Afrikaners—and almost always had combs sticking out of their knee-length dark green socks…
- Hairy underarms or hairy legs on girls or women—an unforgivable sin against good taste and good fashion
- Men who didn't wear sideburns when they were the height of fashion for men
- Men who continued to wear sideburns when that style was passé
- Men who wore rings on their pinky fingers
- Men who wore any kind of jewelry
- Men who wore white shoes – such as my detested orthodontist who had

hairy hands, a pinky ring, *and* wore white shoes

- Girls who wore vests instead of bras
- Girls who wore black patent leather shoes and long or short white socks with frills
- Anyone who said "Can I lend your book?" when what they meant was "May I borrow your book?"
- Anyone who said, "Ag shame!" when they saw a baby, meaning "isn't it sweet?"
- Anyone who said, "is it?" pronounced "izz ut?" when they meant, "is that so?"
- Anyone who cocked their pinky finger when they held a cup, spoon or fork
- Anyone who licked their finger before turning the page
- Anyone who had elocution lessons
- Anyone who said "fillum" when they meant "film."

20—AMERICAN AND CANADIAN HOLIDAY

When I was 11, my mother decided it was time for us to visit her sister in Canada. My Aunt Zoë and Uncle Harry and their children had left South Africa for Toronto two years before. So, off we went—first to America and then to Canada, to Toronto.

As soon as Mom told me about the holiday I began to look forward to it—and the two weeks off school I would have at the end, so it would be a long enough time overseas to make it worth going all that way.

It became more exciting than usual to tear off each passing day on the Sally Worm. Towards the end of each term you would make a Sally Worm out of folded and cut pieces of paper with a smiling worm's face on one end. You wrote the date on each circle of the worm and at the end of each day, you tore off the circle with that day's number on it. The Sally Worms seemed to make the holidays come sooner.

At long last there was only Sally's face left. That meant it was the last day of term. In an hour or two, the holidays would begin.

The girls in my class were very envious, and made me promise to bring them back presents from overseas. My parent's friends came round with going-away gifts, just as they did when I went to England. They brought travel soap and a soft silk pouch to put my jewellery in and some American money.

Mom and I went first to Cape Cod, where we joined up with Zoë and her family.

In Cape Cod, an old woman whom everyone called "Ant Ethel," asked me about South Africa. "Are there monkeys swinging through the trees in *Joe*hannesburg?"

I burst out laughing – I couldn't believe that she really thought there were monkeys swinging through the trees in Johannesburg! Except at the zoo in their cages, of course!

I learned how to play miniature golf, and played so often and so well that I won more free games than I could use up in the time we were there. I went square dancing in bare feet on a hard wooden floor one night and could not walk properly for two days afterwards. And I spoke to my cousin Oliver on the phone when he went back to Toronto, before I joined him there.

"Oliver, stop talking in that strange way! Where did you get that accent like thick soup?"

It didn't take me long to pick up a 'thick soup' Canadian accent of my own when I stayed on in Toronto for a few weeks with my aunt and uncle and went to Don Mills Junior High with Oliver.

My aunt lived in the suburbs, far from the centre of Toronto. Her street had the strange name of Cicada Court. The school was a short walk from her house, across a busy street and a field.

There were two great things about Junior High; it was co-ed, and you didn't have to wear a uniform, just ordinary clothes.

And there was something odd. Almost every girl at the school of about my age was called some version of my name —Kate, Katy, Kathy, Catherine, Cathleen, Kathryn— but mostly Cathy. In South Africa, Cathy was quite an unusual and distinctive name.

I fell in love with a handsome boy called Jon, blond-haired and brown-eyed. Jonny was running for class president. I made a poster for his campaign. It read: "Grade Eight goes Great with Jon-Jon at the Wheel!" and had a picture of a racing car underneath.

We played spin the bottle one night at a party at Oliver's house, in the dark in the basement. I hoped that when I spun the bottle it would land facing Jonny so he would have to kiss me. But it never did and he didn't.

In Canada, I discovered two things you couldn't get in South Africa—a fizzy drink called 'Wink.' and Crest toothpaste. I went to Centre Island and fell off the little train that puttered round the island when I was showing off to Jonny that I could jump on and off the train without falling. I played lots of ping pong in Zoë's basement.

I auditioned for the choir at Temple Emanuel, the synagogue where my aunt and cousins went, and felt very proud when I heard the choir mistress saying to my aunt, "Cathy has a beautiful singing voice. We would love to have her in the choir." And I attended ballet lessons at a dance studio across the park from my aunt's house, dancing en pointe to the envy and admiration of all my girl cousins.

My other 'Canadian' aunt, Helaine, who was married to my uncle Leon, also lived in Don Mills. Sometimes we went over to see them, but their children were much younger than me, so I spent most of the time at Cicada Court. Mom took me and all the cousins who were old enough—Oliver and Lucy and Candy and Sally, and Helaine's oldest daughter, Amanda—to a restaurant to have pancakes with maple syrup and sausages. I wasn't sure if I liked this strange mixture of sweet and savoury that I had never tasted before.

Toronto was full of firsts. It was my first experience, since the age of eight, with a co-ed school. Also, I had my first experience of typing and French – both impossibly difficult, especially when I tried not to look at the keyboard when I typed or when the teacher pounced on me to ask me to say the date or the days of the week in French, which I'd never studied before. I had only heard it pronounced at ballet by Miss de Ville for the steps we danced.

I went bowling for the first time—not the lawn bowling that old men and women played in South Africa, but bowling in an indoor bowling alley in Don Mills. You had to put on special shoes and your aim had to be very good if you wanted to knock any of the pins down.

I made friends with twins called Naomi and Judy, and travelled all by myself on the subway to meet them in Rosedale. In South Africa, I would never have been allowed to go anywhere on my own. It was far too dangerous. I was rather nervous about the expedition, even though Zoë had gone over and over the directions with me, and explained exactly where I had to change trains. By the time I got home to her house that evening, I was very proud of myself, because I had found my way there and all the way back.

I flew back to South Africa, via London, on my own, neatly labelled around the neck as 'unaccompanied child'. Despite the label, I felt very grown up and quite the world traveller.

When I got home to South Africa, I couldn't wait to show to show off my Canadian accent, with its 'aggs' for eggs and its rolling Rs. But the other girls teased it out of me within a week of being back at school in Johannesburg.

But there was something I brought back from Canada that lasted much much longer. No one knew about it so no one could tease me about it. My aunt had taken a photo of Oliver and Jonny and given it to me as a souvenir of my holiday. For at least a year after I got home, I took the photo out of its hiding place beneath my pillow and said good night to them both every night before I went to sleep, and whispered "Hi, sigh guys! Wish I was in Canada with you."

I also recited the names of all the people whose names I could remember from my class at Don Mills Junior High and asked a blessing on them when I said the "*Shmah*" that Grampa had taught me.

"God bless Cameron, Cam, Kim, Kimberley, Kathy, Kathleen, Bill, Catherine, Judy, Naomi, Hilary, Jonny, Oliver …"

21—HOUSES

My first house was Number 2 St. John's Road, on the corner of St. John's Road and Duff Road, in Houghton. Opposite it on Duff Road was the nursery school. Behind us, in a house backing onto Louis Botha Avenue, lived a Greek girl of my age and her family of women, including mother, grandmothers, and aunts. Across the street on St. John's Road was the house where my mother had gone to nursery school in the basement.

My house was officially called Stonecrest. That's what the tarnished brass nameplate outside the front gate said. But nobody ever used that name. It was always called Number 2.

Number 2 had many terraces of lawns, including the swing lawn, the front lawn, the side lawn, the back lawn, and the lawn at the bottom of the garden. That was the one with the best mulberry tree in the world, and a gate to a lane leading to a steep flight of steps to Louis Botha Avenue.

All kinds of trees grew in this garden—peaches, pears, figs, mulberries, walnuts, bell'ombre, and syringa.

I crashed into the walnut tree the first time I tried to ride a bike with foot brakes instead of the handbrakes

MOM ON THE STEPS LEADING UP TO THE POOL TERRACE AT 72 HOUGHTON DR. MATTHEW, BOTTOM RIGHT.

I was used to. My grandmother May gave me first aid by pummeling the bruise to make it go away.

"Ow, May, stop it! You're hurting me. You're making it worse!"

"No, I'm not, Cathy. You'll see there won't be much swelling tomorrow.

83

Otherwise you'll have a huge purple egg on your head in the morning."

She was quite right. Her treatment hurt horribly, but it worked.

The walnuts, in their thick green skins, were so delicious, if you ever succeeded in peeling and breaking them and then cracking through their wrinkled shells. The fig tree produced hundreds of figs. You watched them turn from green to purple, and then quickly picked them before the birds or the moths or the worms got there first. You had to be very careful about eating fresh figs, pulling them open to make sure there were no insects or mould inside them before you ate them. The other fruit trees didn't seem to be that good at actually producing fruit.

The bell'ombre tree, with its small, pungent, poisonous berries, shaded a large sandpit. We didn't spend too much time there as the sand was always damp, and we were sure the cats used it as a litter box.

We didn't use the front lawn much, except for firework displays on November 5th, which was Dad's birthday. It was also Guy Fawkes Day, so we could have fireworks at our house, or we could go to Old Johanians, a country club which had a huge fireworks display every year on Guy Fawkes Day. But it was always so crowded that, on the whole, we preferred to have our own fireworks. I loved the Catherine Wheels, spinning round, shooting sparks, and the huge Sparklers, which you could wave round to write words in the air. But I was always afraid that a firecracker would land in front of me, or that the shower of coloured lights from a rocket would fall into my hair and set it alight.

We didn't spend much time on the small side lawn next to the garage either, except to greet visitors who drove onto the brick parking spot beside it. But we liked the back lawn with its washing line at one end and its syringa tree with its poisonous clusters of orange berries at the other.

The mulberry tree on the bottom lawn had two purposes. You could gather its fruit in large plastic bowls and eat handfuls of mulberries as you picked. And its leaves were for feeding to silk worms which made amazing patterns on thin sheets of cardboard you cut into interesting shapes. You put the silkworms and their mulberry leaves onto the cardboard in a shoebox, with holes punched in the lid, and waited for them to spin their golden silk over the cardboard pieces. Then you took the box with its writhing contents to school, to show off to your friends, and to see if your silkworms had made more silk than theirs. While they were spinning, strange crunching sounds came from the box.

The laundry room in the back yard at Number 2 was also the servants' bathroom. It was close to the servants' rooms. The family used the bathrooms inside the house. We had two bathrooms, one beside the kitchen for the children, and the other at the opposite end of the house for the grown ups, up a short flight of steps.

One day I locked myself into the grown-ups' bathroom and couldn't unlock the door. I shouted and shouted for help. At last, John, the gardener, put a tall ladder up against the outside wall and climbed in to the bathroom and unlocked the door.

The servants lived in tiny concrete rooms up behind the laundry room, beside the garage. You always had to knock if you wanted to go into their rooms. You were not allowed to just barge in.

My bedroom had a curtained alcove looking onto the back lawn. It had a chest of drawers, and a small cupboard, where clothes and dolls, including the hated cloth doll, Susannah, lived in a heap. Later, after Eliza was born, William and I shared this room, which had a bunk bed in it. I slept on the top bunk. I was the eldest so I got first choice, and the top bunk was what I wanted.

I went through a brief phase of being very tidy. I would fold a sock, open the top drawer of the chest, put the sock in it, close the drawer, then fold the other sock, open the drawer, put that away, and then close the drawer again. Pretty soon I got tired of being so neat, and went back to leaving my clothes in heaps on the floor for the servants to pick up, fold, and tidy away.

**

The family moved to Number 72 Houghton Drive just before Matthew was born. The first thing anyone noticed about the house was its pink carpet in the large L-shaped living room. Next, you noticed the white chandeliers with pink leather roses, and a fancy ironwork and glass door which you locked with an iron bar. The door had a resonant, reassuring clang when you shot the bar home and you knew that no burglar could possibly get through that door without making so much noise that you would have time to call the police, who would catch him before he had a chance to steal anything.

The long part of the L of the living room had a big tall bay window with a C-shaped seat, facing north, which got lots of sunshine and was a perfect spot to doze and read on your tummy, with a cat perched on your back,

NUMBER 72 HOUGHTON DRIVE, LOOKING NORTH. THE BAY WINDOW IS IN THE LIVING ROOM AND HAS THE WONDERFUL WINDOW SEAT. CATHY'S BEDROOM WINDOW IS BESIDE THE SLOPING BEAM ON THE RIGHT.

purring loudly. There was also a fireplace with two cushioned alcoves on either side, and sofas and chairs that got fresh covers every few years. We had lots of prints and paintings on the wall. After a while, we didn't see them any more, till someone new came to the house and noticed and asked about them. The short part of the L housed the gramophone in its squat wooden cabinet and had glass doors leading to patios to the north and east.

Behind the living room was the back room or morning room, as Mom preferred to call it. It held the huge black piano, which my Uncle Arnold had given me when he left to go to England. This room, too, had a fireplace with an iron fire screen used for drying washing in the winter when it was too cold to hang things on the washing line in the backyard. One wall was lined with bookshelves from the floor to the ceiling, and there was a tall bay window to the east. This was a good window for climbing in and out of to get to the side of the garden nearest the swimming pool.

Next to the morning room was the ironing passageway and 'the downstairs loo,' tall and narrow, then the kitchen, which looked onto the concrete of the backyard and the servants' quarters and up the tangled slope of the *kopje*.

Beside the kitchen was a little scullery where my mother or Ellen would trim the flowers they picked from the garden, using sharp secateurs to scrape off the thorns from the roses. The scullery led into the pantry with its locked white cupboard for groceries and its cupboards with china for special occasions, as well as for every day. On a broad ledge sat the tins that held the cakes and biscuits Ellen baked. A door from the scullery went into the dining room with its lovely, big north-facing window overlooking the front lawn and a view to Pretoria, and a big window seat. All rooms that faced north had the same view, over miles of trees. A large, round, light-coloured wooden table stood slightly off-centre, surrounded by cast iron chairs, very pointed and modern, with brightly-coloured square cushions. There was a small fireplace, in working order, but never lit. A glass door led to the study, where my parents had their desks and typewriters and kept the family documents, neatly arranged.

The back door of the study led to a double garage. This was later turned into a large family room with a huge yellow-wood table and underfloor heating, soft rugs, and floor-to-ceiling bookshelves.

Beside the new living room was a courtyard, with brick walls and crisscrossing beams to roof it in with dappled shade, and a lot of greenery and some small pieces of sculpture, including one of a saint from Dad's chambers, brought home when he moved from one set to another.

There were two ways to get out of the courtyard and into the garden. One was via a locked wooden door, which led into the brick carport. The other was through a locked wrought-iron gate that led directly to the side of the house with the bougainvillea. You had to remember to bring the keys with you, and to lock the doors behind you.

Upstairs, off the guest bedroom, was a secret room full of cupboards, with a small window, which looked towards the pool. The window had a large wooden ledge. The door was always locked. Sometimes I sneaked in, taking the key from the basket in my mother's dressing room. The secret room smelled musty, of mothballs, and things that had been forgotten. In the cupboards were clothes that my parents didn't wear anymore – my mother's wedding dress, and an old suit of my father's. There were also my parents' skiing clothes, from when they'd been to Kreifeld in Austria on a winter holiday: navy trousers of strong stretchy material and heavy woollen jerseys, in red and black, and ski masks, with round black holes for the eyes and mouth. There were shelves of china and silver and linen. I hoped, each time I went in there, to find a treasure. But all I found were solitude and mothballs.

This was my favourite room for swotting and for thinking. I knew no one would think of looking for me there, and I could ignore their shouts.

My bedroom had a small fireplace, which was sometimes lit as a special treat, and a large window facing north that looked over the front lawn. My bed was of beautiful light brown wood, with an elegant headboard and matching bedside table. The dressing table, which also served as a desk, had a large mirror on top. My room also had a small box record-player. I listened to the latest Beatles' songs over and over and over till my parents yelled, "For goodness's sake, turn that thing off!"

The evening and morning sounds that I heard from my room were strange and sometimes frightening. There was the one that sounded like heavy-footed burglars rampaging over the roof–but it was only pigeons. And the thumping and bumping sound that could start at any time was just the boiler in the linen cupboard outside my bedroom door. I lived in fear that it would explode one day, drenching William and me in boiling water.

Mom and Dad's bedroom was large, its high bay window facing north with a view over trees and houses stretching for miles into the distance. The floor was wooden parquet in a geometrical pattern. Other windows faced east towards the cricket lawn. A white wicker chair with bright cushions and a matching footstool were ready for reading in or chatting to Mom while she tried to have an afternoon nap. The dressing room, which could be partitioned off with a white bamboo curtain, also faced north and east so was very bright. It had a little window opening onto it from the bathroom, which led off the bedroom.

The dressing room contained a wooden stand for Dad's suits, and one chest of drawers for his shirts and socks and underwear. My mother had a whole row of white cupboards and drawers for her things. I paid secret visits to the dressing room and went through the drawers and cupboards, looking at things and sometimes trying them on, when my mother was out or busy elsewhere in the house. I took great care to replace the things neatly so my visits would not be discovered.

The drawers contained: underwear neatly folded into pretty cotton bags; jewellery in a locked cupboard, but I knew where to find the key; and lots of handbags and scarves and blouses. Other drawers were full of make-up, such as vivid lipsticks when bright colour was the fashion, and pale, pearly colours when it was their turn. There was a stool to sit on and an oval mirror with a pale golden frame, where you could see how the various shades of red or orange or pink suited you. To make yourself feel even more grownup and beautiful, you could squirt yourself with Mom's favourite French perfume, 'Y Greque' by Yves St. Laurent...

My favourite things to try on were Mom's jewellery and shoes. Mom had the most beautiful collection of beads, necklaces, rings, and brooches. The less valuable ones were on display in various baskets and boxes, things of beauty in themselves. The jewellery made of real diamonds and pearls and garnets were in the locked drawers.

The shoes were of every colour and style: evening sandals with sparkles, and daytime sandals with buckles and flowers, or just plain white leather, and dark court shoes with flat black bows. Hidden at the back of the cupboard were Mom's silver wedding shoes with their platform-soles. Each time I tried on her shoes, I hoped that *this* time I would find a pair of shoes that fitted my feet. But somehow, none of them ever looked or felt quite right on me.

The big cupboard in the dressing room also held Mom's dresses, and on the top shelf was a collection of hats. These were harder to reach. To try them on, I had to get permission and help from her to hand them down to me.

At the top of the stairs over the front door was the suitcase cupboard, with its musty, unused smell of old leather and worn-out cloth suitcases. But it was not as pungent as the cupboard under the stairs, which smelled of linseed oil from the cricket bats, untreated wood from the tennis racquet frames, old tennis balls, and shiny red cricket balls.

Doors from William's and my bedrooms led to the playroom with its bookshelves, low cupboards for toys, and a tall cupboard for storing Mom's sewing things and my old ballet costumes. The playroom had the barre for ballet practice. When we got the new gramophone, the old boxy wooden one came upstairs and scratched our Beatles records. The playroom also had a pingpong table, which was not quite standard-sized. From the playroom windows, we could look out to see who was arriving. But we had an even better view from the porch windows. However, you had to be sure to shut the curtains if you were getting dressed in there, or the coal men carrying sacks of coal up and down the drive could look up and see you in your underwear.

The house was perched half way up a hill at the top of a steep stone drive. The drive's hairpin bend and uneven surface were the terror of guests, family, and deliverymen, whose cars and vans groaned and complained, sputtering and choking as they struggled to reach the top. If you were driving, you needed to shift into lowest gear and then put your foot to the floor and rush up the drive in a burst of speed before you or your car had time to think about the treachery of the drive. It was tackled only by the bravest and most determined visitors. When there were big parties, the guests parked in the street and we hired a special driver to take them up to the house if they didn't want to walk.

The pine kopje behind the house was a no-go territory for me. It was the haunt of the boys who lived in the boarding house of King Edward School at the top of the kopje and who might be smoking and doing who knew what else on the kopje. They terrorized my brothers going home from school. The boarders regarded our kopje and garden as their right of way and shortcut to Old Eds, the sports club connected to the school, which was about a mile or so down the road from our house. Cutting through the kopje and down through our garden saved the boarders about 20 minutes or more in getting to Old Eds.

The rest of the outside areas of the house felt safe—the terraced lawns, with their flowers and shrubs. At this house, besides the front lawn, we had the swing lawn, the cricket lawn with the huge bell'ombre on one side of it, and the patio beside the pool. A huge compost heap hidden behind the bell'ombre was fed by Joseph, the gardener, when he felt like working.

The rectangular swimming pool was above the side lawn on the east side of the house at the foot of the kopje. Its walls were painted white and had a border of tiny, brightly coloured mosaic tiles, and it had a fountain of brass pipes and brick at the shallow end. The white walls made the water pale blue, very different from the bright blue of my friends' swimming pools. The change rooms and pool equipment were in round brick buildings, one with a roof, one roofless, that looked like the elephant houses at the zoo. The brick patio beside them had a beamed trellis with a Catawba grape vine that Dad's friend George pruned each year. Mom made the grapes into a most delicious jam, perfect for spreading on scones.

On the cricket lawn, Dad and William played cricket. Sometimes I joined in when it was French cricket and they were using a tennis ball instead of a cricket ball. We also played badminton there. Sometimes, my leaps and arabesques won me a game, but more often, they earned teasing from William as he lobbed a shuttlecock just out of reach of my racquet from the baseline on his side of the net.

22—PLAYING THE PIANO

In the back room downstairs at Number 72 stood an enormous, beautiful upright piano, an Ibach, black and shining. Its voice was deep and melodious in the lower keys and sweet and shrill in the upper keys. It had been my uncle Arnold's piano. He gave it to me when I was four years old, when he and my Aunt Marian left South Africa forever to live in England. Arnold was a musician who had written the words and music for many songs. He did not want to take the huge piano with him on the boat all the way to London.

"I will buy another one when I get to England. I want you to have this piano and learn to play it well because I can tell you love music."

So from the age of four, I played the piano. Whenever I heard a tune that I liked on the gramophone or the radio or that someone was singing, I rushed to the piano to try to pick it out with one finger, and later, with chords. I was very pleased with myself when it sounded right.

Before he left, Arnold taught me how to clean the piano. You washed the keys with a cloth dipped in milk, making sure to wring out the cloth so the liquid would not drip down into the recesses of the keyboard and curdle and stink up the instrument. The piano made strange plunking noises as you washed first the black keys and then the ivories.

And Arnold told me not to forget to have the piano tuned once a year. So Mom or Dad would phone the blind piano tuner and he would come with his tuning fork and instruments and stand pinging and tinging and twiddling and adjusting for hours. And when he had finished, everything sounded better—even the wrong notes.

My official piano lessons began when I was about six with Miss Sini van den Brom. She lived in Auckland Park, very near my school. Once a week, I went to her house after school for lessons. Miss van den Brom was from Holland and had blonde hair in a bun. The lessons took place in a cool, shady room with large windows. There was a special kind of smell in her house, of Dutch biscuits that she had baked, or of lemon and ginger. I liked the way her voice sounded, speaking English in a foreign way.

My piano book had pictures and words to go with the music. There were "Bells are ringing hearts are singing" by Beethoven and "How much wood could a woodchuck chuck if a woodchuck could chuck wood?" by anon.

My next teacher, whom I went to for many years, was Mrs. Lola Porter. She lived in a big house in Houghton, not too far from ours. Mrs. Porter did not make her pupils go in for exams, recitals, or theory.

I managed to study piano and make good progress, acquiring a reasonable technique, without bothering much about key signatures, but bothering quite a lot about marks of expression and tempi.

MOM AND CATHY (AGED 3) AT THE BEACH AT PLETTENBERG BAY.

Mrs. Porter expected you to play well because you loved the piano, not because there was a performance or trial on the horizon. I was terrified enough of ballet exams, from which there was no escape; but the very thought of a piano exam filled me with panic. Even playing in front of my family, if they came into the back room when I was practising, turned my fingers immediately into wooden blocks.

That didn't happen very often, though, because I hated practising. I would come home from school knowing that I had a piano lesson that evening, and that I also had a sack full of homework, including maths and science. I was dismal at both these subjects. The battle would begin almost immediately.

"Cathy, I haven't heard you practising the piano lately, and your lesson is in an hour. Go and practise."

"I won't, Mom. I can't. I have too much homework. I'll practise *after* the lesson."

"Then you'd better start on your maths. I wasn't too happy with the mark you got on your last test."

I ran into the backroom, slammed the door and sat down on the wooden piano bench, opened up Hanon's "The Virtuoso Pianist" and began to rush through the endless, repetitive exercises up and down the piano. I hoped this would make my fingers flexible enough that "Lola" wouldn't notice how little time I had spent on the Mozart sonata I was supposed to have practised.

Actually, practising or not practising the piano was a strange business. Often I would come to a lesson feeling guilty for not having practised enough and Lola would praise my playing, making me feel even more guilty. And then on the days when I had practised and practised, my fingers would sound wooden and I would be scolded for not having practised enough.

"Cathy, you have a gift for piano. You're wasting it by not practising," she said, looking at me reproachfully over her spectacles.

When I was 13, I had to choose between piano lessons and ballet lessons, because the long hours of school at Roedean did not allow for both, so I dropped piano and carried on briefly with ballet.

But I continued to pick out tunes, and to accompany myself when I was learning a song by picking out the top line of the music. My favourites were the classical pieces that I heard at my ballet classes—Chopin and Schubert especially, played by Melanie of the straight orange hair and large glasses. And Schubert's Grand March from *Lilac Time*, or waltzes from the ballets *Swan Lake* or *Copelia*. Ballet was my introduction to many pieces of classical music.

Most of the time the piano stood in its appointed place in the backroom, growing older and more neglected with each passing day. It came to life once in a while when William's friend Chorbs came over.

You couldn't keep Chorbs away from a piano. "Chorbs" got his nickname because he had the worst acne in the world. But you forgot all about this when he played. His playing was astonishing, and he had never had a lesson in his life. He could play by ear anything he heard.

When he played Simon & Garfunkel's *Bridge over Troubled Waters* it made you want to weep with its beauty, and gnash your teeth in envy and frustration because you knew you would *never* be able to play so well.

And sometimes the piano would be used when my father's cousin Bertie, the singer, visited. He and I always went into the backroom to test his perfect pitch. He sang in the choir at shule.

"Are you ready? I will turn my back on the piano and you can play any note you like and I will tell you what it is."

So I would play a C or a G sharp or a B flat. It didn't matter where I played it or how quickly I moved from one note to the next, I could never outwit Bertie.

MOM AND DAD

23—NAMES

The first time you hear a name or the first person you meet with a particular name gives that name the shape and feel it will have forever.

Take David. How could anyone like a name that belonged to a pale warty boy who pulled your hair and dipped it into the inkwell on his desk and stuffed itchy balls down your back?

There were lots of exotic names among my friends whose parents came from Norway or Sweden—Priscilla, Annika, Prunella, and Kari. And APPS had also brought me Miss Merlin Carter—and what name could be lovelier than that?

I loved the name Bosky, which belonged to Ellen's son. He was very often spoken of, but hardly ever seen, and was about my age.

Then there was the name that my parents would tease me with, saying, "We were going to call you Tatiana, but decided not to, at the last minute." Actually, I knew they had really wanted to name me "Emma," after the Jane Austen heroine in the book that Dad read to us when we were older. But Grampa, my mother's father, had said, "Emma is a servant's name and I won't have any grandchild of mine given that name." So my mother, who was otherwise very strong-willed, agreed to call her first child Catherine Emma Helen (after Grampa's mother, whom she had not particularly cared for).

Most of the time I detested my long name, Catherine. This was because of the Scottish French teacher at Roedean, who called us all by our full names. There was no Vicky or Cathy, Jenny, or Nicky or Maz in her class. There were only Catherine, Victoria, Jennifer, Nicola, and Marion. Perhaps we might have liked our full names, once we got used to them. But she was the only one who used them, and the way she said "Catherine" ruined the name for me.

"Catherine Kentridge. Six out of ten, again! Six is such a wishy-washy mark. I think I am going to faint!"

But we were more likely to faint than she was – from the overpowering reek of the cheroots she chain-smoked in the staffroom and which followed her into the classroom in a smelly cloud.

Lovely Miss Larraine De Ville, my ballet teacher, called me "Catherine" and made it sound beautiful, but she was a part of my life long before my French teacher, and I had almost forgotten how she said it.

There was something about the various French teachers at my school and names—not just how they said ours, but also the names they gave their own daughters—Ailsa Violet, Deborah Mary, Anthea, Delia—what had those girls done to deserve such dire names?   But although we felt it was very hard on them to have such names, we could not resist making fun of them any time we got the chance.

Russell was a name I liked a lot, and Donald. I had a crush on a boy called Russell when I was seven or eight. He had brown hair and large brown eyes and was in class at Auckland Park till the end of Grade Two. Donald was in my cousin Oliver's class at KEPS (King Edward VII Preparatory School). He was 10 years old, and I met him one Sports Day. He was wearing a pink rosette, his house colour, and white shorts and shirt. For months afterwards I imagined situations where I saved his life, or looked after him with tender devotion in hospital. Luckily for me, Donald and Oliver didn't know of this passion, or they would have teased the life out of me.

My mother's name, Felicia, was so beautiful and unusual. It means "happiness." My mother had been born a short while after a terrible tragedy struck the family. A cousin called Miriam, a wonderful sculptor, had died in an accident. She was living with my grandparents and my Aunt Zoë. One day Miriam was in the bathroom doing some ironing with a benzene-filled iron. The iron exploded and she was burnt to death. Zoë told me that my grandmother Irene had a nervous breakdown after the death of Miriam, and had never fully recovered. The new baby was intended to bring joy back into her life again, and certainly did for her big sister and her father. But my mother told me that she could never recall her mother laughing and happy as people said she used to be before Miriam's accident.

My mother's family continued to live in the house after the accident, and it was the very same house I lived in till I was 11.

My family was very particular about how names were pronounced. Felicia was pronounced "Felisha," as in Patricia, and anyone who dared to say "FeLEEseea" or worse still, "feLEEsha," incurred the wrath of everyone in the family. Another faux pas was to say "Ireen" when you were talking to or about my grandmother Irene. Didn't people know the proper pronunciation was "Ireenee?"

My parents, grandparents, aunts, and uncles always called me Cathy, never Catherine. And they always called my sister "Eliza," never Elizabeth. It was just the opposite with my brothers. No one ever thought of calling William "Billy" or "Willy" or "Bill" or "Will." And my youngest brother, Matthew, was always called by his full name.

Much as we all adore our father, William, Eliza, Matthew, and I have always regarded his name, Sydney, as being beyond the pale. Dad says he agrees with us. I think my grandmother May had a terrible taste in names. She named her sons Sydney Woolf, Arnold Godfrey, and Leon Ross. Later, when someone explained to me that the names were chosen to honour various ancestors, I still felt that May inflicted unnecessary hardship on her sons by labelling them with those names. Family legend—fiercely defended by my father and my uncle Arnold—says that she had to be talked out of giving the name "Rose" to her youngest son as his middle name. The "Rose" was changed to "Ross."

Leslie and Sheila, identical twins, slim with short reddish brown hair, freckles covering every inch of skin, and pierced ears with thin gold hoops, convinced me that those names could only belong to thin freckled girls. The twins were adopted, something I regarded as very exotic. One day they arrived at school with the exciting news that their mother had had a little girl, called Dawn, who very soon acquired pierced ears of her own. The family lived in one of the new duplexes in Hyde Park, the latest thing. I thought they were much nicer than my large house with its huge gardens in Houghton. The twins' mother used to cook up "Egyptian Toffee" in a huge pot on the top of her stove. The smell was rich, sweet and cloying. At first I thought it was some kind of sweet and wondered why she never offered us a taste when I came over to play at their house. It was only when the twins explained that the "toffee" was a special kind of wax that, once heated, you used to take the hair off your legs, that I was very relieved we had not tried to eat it.

William's schools had the most unusual names and nicknames for the teachers. But Roedean won hands down with the names of its pupils:

Pandora, Rowena, Keithayn, Mymie, Dairin, Heidi, Marissa, Peta, Xanthe, and of course, Deborah Mary, Ailsa Violet, Delia, and Anthea. I think with "Catherine" I got off lightly.

But the strangest and funniest name of all belonged to the boy in an old school photograph of Dad's. In the back row, his face round and smiling, stood "Beefy Schmulian."

24—WORDS AND PRONUNCIATION

Baking Soda: I was very confused by a recipe for Honeycomb in an issue of *Princess*, the girls' magazine that I received by surface mail once a month from England (so it was too late to enter the competitions by the specified closing date, which had always long since passed by the time the magazine reached Johannesburg.) The crucial ingredient was 'baking soda'. We didn't have any baking soda in the house. We had 'bicarbonate of soda' and we had 'baking powder'. Which one did the recipe mean? I tried the recipe several times, and finally worked out that you got honeycomb when you used bicarbonate of soda, and a sticky, bad-tasting mess when you used 'baking powder'.

Chaffed: "He chaffed me he had R100 in the bank" – (pronounced "charfed"). He pretended he had 100 rands in the bank.

Chauffeur: The African, in a smart jacket and cap, whom rich families hired to drive them around. Pronounced "Chorefur."

Chocolate mousse: Another confusing recipe in *Princess*. This one was for *Chocolate mousse*, which I pronounced as chocolate mouse. I could not understand why the recipe didn't describe how to shape the concoction into a mouse-like shape.

Coppertone: The advertisements for this suntan lotion had a drawing of a child with a bathing suit and a dog pulling it down at one side so you could see the brown of the child's skin was from using Coppertone, and that underneath she was really a little white child.

Dur: A term of opprobrium, to describe someone you thought was wet or pathetic. "Clare is such a dur. I wish I didn't have to share a study with her."

Fouetté: A French ballet word, pronounced "foytay" by my ballet teachers.

Golliwogs: Golliwog dolls were not allowed in our house. I didn't mind because I thought they were very ugly, with their round black faces, short woolly hair, smiling red mouths, and bright button eyes. And I didn't like their jackets and striped trousers either. My parents banned golliwogs because they said the dolls made fun of non-whites.

Hairybacks: A vulgar and offensive word used by some English-speaking white South Africans to refer to Afrikaners.

Kaffir: The most offensive and insulting name a white person could use to refer to an African, as in "These bloody kaffirs, they're all the same. Can't trust them as far as you can kick them." Usage absolutely forbidden in our house.

Lekker: An Afrikaans word used by all English–speaking South Africans as well. It meant you had enjoyed something very much. "We had a lekker time at the zoo," or "That film was lekker" or "That cake was lekker."

Lovey: A word Grampa used to express his love for his grandchildren. We despised it. But if my ballet teacher Miss De Ville called me "Lovey," it was just fine.

Née: Something you read in the births or marriages announcements, pronounced "knee."

Pumping custard: As in "my heart pumps custard for you that you only have three pairs of sandals and not five," meaning in a sarcastic way "I'm so sorry for you."

Reader's Digest: A magazine whose title was beyond me. I had no idea what it had to do with food, and pronounced it "Readers digest." Grampa was a subscriber and we would work our way through the "It pays to increase your Word Power" section together.

Retirés: A French ballet word, which my ballet teachers pronounced as "Reterrays"

Rock Spiders or Rocks: Vulgar and offensive words used by some English-speaking white South Africans to refer to Afrikaners.

Rooineks: An insulting word used by some Afrikaners to refer to English-speaking white South Africans. Literally "red necks." Originally it referred to the British soldiers whose fair skin burned in the South African sun.

Sandshoes: The word Dad used for what we called "tackies" (running shoes).

Sea and Ski: A suntanning lotion – I always thought it was a 'cute' way of spelling sky and pronounced it as "sky."

Sies!: Used when something said, seen, heard, touched, or tasted was disgusting. It was pronounced "Sis."

Smaak: An Afrikaans word, which we misused. "I smaak that chocolate cake" meaning a combination of "I'd like a piece" and "it tastes very good."

Spaz: A term of opprobrium. "She's such a spaz, she still wears socks instead of pantyhose."

Stompie: The Afrikaans word for a cigarette stub. Used in the expression, "Don't pick up stompies," when someone tries to butt in on a conversation, not having heard the beginning.

Tackies: The word used by every South African, whatever their home language, for running shoes.

Taz: As in "that dress is taz," meaning great.

Tit: As in "that was a really tit song" meaning it was a very good song.

Wogs: An offensive name some of the girls at my schools called non-whites.

THE BOTTOM PART OF THE DRIVE AT NUMBER 72 HOUGHTON DRIVE,
JACARANDA TREES IN BLOSSOM.

25—BEING JEWISH

Grampa was endlessly good-natured and loving, and did his best to teach us about the things that he felt were most important, such as being Jewish, and mathematics.

It was hard to be Jewish in a community of Anglicans. My parents had made a deliberate decision not to send us to Jewish schools.

"Those schools make you think you're better than other people and different from them. And it gives you a much smaller circle of friends."

So my sister and I were sent to Anglican schools, where we were among a handful of Jewish girls, but my brothers went to the local public school where there were lots of other Jewish boys.

For them, staying home for the Jewish holidays, even if they didn't go to shul, was a gesture of solidarity and not just a religious matter. For me and Eliza, staying home for Yom Kippur, Rosh Hashanah or Pesach, was awkward and embarrassing, leading to bitchy remarks from the other girls who had not "had the day off school like you Jews."

The hardest times were Easter and Christmas. The schools I went to had assembly every morning with prayers and hymns. At Easter all the hymns were about crucifixion. They made my blood run cold, and I was convinced that all the girls were pointing their fingers at me and blaming me for the cruelty and horror of the crucifixion. I stood in the hall during these daily ordeals, my head down, sort of singing the hymns—enjoying the music, but leaving out lots of words—such as any mention of "Jesus" or "Crucified."

**

I'd first become aware of being Jewish, and therefore different, when I was at Auckland Park and had been given a talking to by the headmistress for taunting a Chinese girl at the school. Mrs. Gilham had made me realize how much I would hate being called "Jew, Jew Jewess."

I'd never thought about being Jewish before. Now I started to feel embarrassed.

It did not get better as the round of Christian religious holidays turned through the year. Christmas was the only time I wanted to be Christian like everyone around me, so I could read a lesson for the Lessons and Carols Service. I knew I was by far the best reader in the school, but I was not allowed to participate because I was Jewish.

The only good thing was that I was excused carol practice with the neurotic singing teacher, seeing I would not be attending the carol service, "because you are Jewish."

**

At home, we did not keep kosher and hardly ever attended synagogue, except on Yom Kippur, or a for a brief period when Grampa took us to shul on Friday nights. But we did celebrate the High Holidays such as Pesach, Rosh Hashanah, Yom Kippur, and Chanukah with feast or fasting or candle-lighting as the occasion required. So we associated these holidays with eating certain foods or not being allowed to eat certain foods rather than with anything religious. My mother and father had both told me, at different times, that they had had far too much religion inflicted on them in their childhood to inflict it on us.

Grampa was the only one who paid any attention to our religious or Jewish upbringing and education. He taught us about Pesach, Chanukah, Rosh Hashanah, and Yom Kippur, and on each holiday, he offered prizes to all grandchildren who wrote essays about that particular religious holiday. The prize was usually 10 Rands and a book about Judaism.

My favourite was a book of biographies of *Great Jewish Men of the 19th and 20th Centuries*. The book did not talk about their religious beliefs but about their childhoods and their achievements. As he gave me the book, inscribed "To Cathy for her essay on Chanukah, 1965," he said, "Lovey, this book will tell you about the great men of our people so that you can feel proud to be a Jew."

"Grampa, please tell us a story about some famous Jewish people you knew."

And Grampa would sit down and tell us about Ben Gurion, who was the first Prime Minister of the State of Israel, which had been founded in

1948, and Theodore Herzl, who founded the Zionist movement and other men who had been courageous pioneers in Israel.

**

Grampa was a walking encyclopedia of South African Jewry. You could mention any name that you had heard or read about in the papers, and Grampa could tell you all about that person's family, circumstances and career, and whether he thought that person was good or bad. In the years leading up to the Second World War, Grampa had saved many German Jews from certain death by bringing them to South Africa and safety.

Grampa had very strong views generally about who and what was good and who and what was bad. He could not speak with any calmness about the British. "They betrayed us in Palestine. They broke their promises, they helped our enemies," he said, grinding his teeth and shaking his fist.

And at synagogue, where he sometimes took me and Oliver and William on Friday evenings, he would become enraged if he thought the rabbi was being bigoted, wrong-headed, or simply had a different point of view. I hated going to shul because it was the Orthodox shul where the women sat upstairs, separated from the men. You had to lean far over the balcony to even see the men. And only men and boys were allowed to sing in the choir. The women and girls around me, all dressed in their very best, never smiled or nodded, still less exchanged a word with me during the endless hours. The service was conducted almost entirely in Hebrew, and as I didn't read or understand Hebrew, I tried to make the time go by reading the English parts of the prayer book. If I got bored with that, I could look around me and notice what everyone was wearing. But mostly I spent my time wishing and wishing the rabbi would finish his sermon, liberally sprinkled with Hebrew quotations and exhortations, and that the cantor would finish his whining and that the men would finish their dovening so that we could all go home to "Ga's flat" for Friday night supper.

Before or after dinner, Grampa would quiz us on the sermon and then we would listen to Howard Greenspan's "Stars of Tomorrow" on the radio.

**

Grampa's other efforts to teach me about being Jewish were doomed to failure. He tried to teach me to write and read Hebrew. He tried making it enjoyable, explaining what the letters on the Dreidel meant, and how unusual and fun it was to read from right to left instead of left to right. He was endlessly patient. It was no use. I was sulky and stubbornly reluctant to

105

learn. In the end he gave up and concentrated on my brother William, who at least showed some willingness to learn and also had a much sweeter disposition.

But there was one time of the year when I was quite happy to learn about being Jewish and even to try to master some Hebrew or Aramaic. And that was Pesach. I enjoyed writing essays about the exodus from Egypt. Oliver and I, as the eldest grandchildren, didn't have any chance of doing solos at the Seder of the Four Questions in Aramaic. We had to leave that to William and Lucy, but we learnt the words anyway, and we sang the songs loudly and vigorously. I loved some of the special food: the charoset and the *kneidlach* and the matzo. I didn't care for the *gefilte fish* or the chopped herring, and was happy to donate my shares to William. I had an absolute horror of horseradish, especially the magenta kind, as I was convinced it was made from minced horses. It was years before I could even bring myself to taste it. Best of all was eating the matzo and hunting for or hiding the Afikomen. Actually, we preferred to do the hiding and then have Grampa pays its ransom in cash or books.

**

Being Jewish also meant you had to be very careful when you were invited to a "Christian" place such as the Johannesburg Country Club. The first time one of my friends invited me to go swimming there with her family, she said, "You know Jews aren't allowed at the club, but we won't tell them you're Jewish."

I was sure I looked very Jewish, and that all the Anglicans at the club would be able to see this at once So all afternoon beside the swimming pool, I kept my sunglasses on and my head down, with occasional frightened glances around to see if one of the officers or guests at the club was striding angrily towards me, having found out I was Jewish, and would loudly and angrily order me to leave.

But it never happened, and every night I wrapped myself in prayer before I went to sleep, saying aloud the words Grampa had taught me:

"*Shma Yisrael, Adonai Eloheinu Adonia Ehad.* Hear O Israel, the Lord our God, the Lord is One."

26—BALLET

I knew that I had been born to dance. Why else would I find the smell of used ballet slippers so intoxicating and redolent of beauty and magic?

I went to dancing lessons from the age of six. First, to a strange man who taught me Greek dancing in a studio somewhere far from home. But that didn't last for very long. For his lessons I wore a white tunic and had bare feet.

Then I discovered Royal Academy ballet.

Lovely Miss Larraine De Ville was my first ballet teacher. Miss De Ville had short, dark hair and a sweet smile, and hands that were so soft holding your rough, wintry, dried-out hands that you didn't ever want to let go. For classes she wore Lycra stretch trousers, twinsets, and black ballet slippers with pink elastic across the instep.

Dad loved to tease me about her name. "How was your class with Mister Ville today? Was he wearing ballet shoes?"

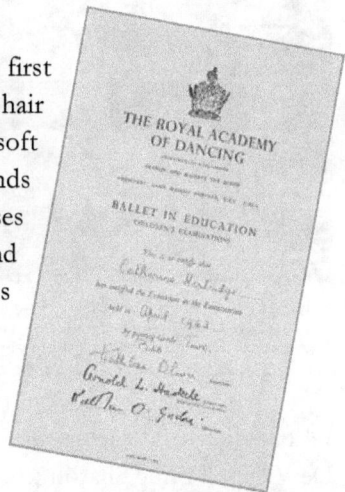

"Daddy, you know it's *Miss* de Ville. I've told you and told you!" I said.

A CERTIFICATE SHOWING WHAT USUALLY HAPPENED IN BALLET EXAMS—PASSING GRADE 2.

Second only in my heart to Miss Larraine De Ville was her sister, Miss Denise. Miss Denise was 14 and had the starring roles in the ballet shows. She was Snow White and I was a doe with a brown velvet costume, and a little hat with antlers, in one of the few ballet competitions in which my mother allowed me to participate.

107

My mother had no time for the "Ballet Moms" who sat around with heavily dyed hair, brightly painted fingernails and electric green eye shadow, loudly chewing gum and criticizing as they watched us dance.

"Mom, *please* come and see me dance. Miss De Ville thinks I'm very good. I really want you to see me dance," I said.

"Cathy, I will not sit and listen to those women gossiping and making nasty remarks all through class. I just won't do it," she said.

My tears and pleas fell on deaf ears.

I'd wait a few weeks and then try again, hoping this time she would agree to come. Surely if my mother ever saw me at a ballet class she would find something to praise?

"Cathy, I've told you I won't come, and I haven't changed my mind," she said.

One wonderful day when I was about 11, Miss De Ville called me up to her in front of the whole class. "Cathy, you are dancing so beautifully. Would you like a solo in the Concorde Competition in October?"

THE PRIMA BALLERINA ASSOLUTA IN TRAINING AT THE TERRACE BESIDE THE SWIMMING POOL—WITH THE BALLERINA BUN, COURTESY OF SARI NEXT DOOR.

Would I like a solo? Would I *like* a solo?

"Oh, yes please, please, thank you," I stammered, smiling so hard my face ached.

The other girls looked sick with envy. I'd overheard their mothers beg and threaten Miss De Ville.

"If you don't give Beverley a solo, I'll take her to a teacher who appreciates her talent." Or "Ag please, Miss De Ville, I'll bring Sharon to extra lessons," they said.

Sometimes I could see they had worn her down and she gave in.

When Mom came to fetch me, I could hardly wait to get into the car before I burst out, "Miss De Ville offered me a solo in Concorde. I would be *en pointe* and it would be to a Chopin Prelude." I began to hum the music.

"Let's get this straight. I'm *not* having you compete in Concorde, so we won't even talk about it again," she said.

When I got home, Ellen saw my tears. She put her arms around me and promised to make my favourite supper of grilled lamb chops and her special thin crisp chips. But I couldn't eat. The food stuck in my throat.

"There there, it's not so bad, my darling. Don't cry," she said, over and over. But I couldn't stop, and I cried myself to sleep.

**

Although I was not allowed to compete i~~n the~~ Concorde or the Eisteddfod, the other great ballet competition i~~n~~ Johannesburg, I was allowed to do ballet exams—~~a~~ source of torment and frustration.

At the rehearsals, even up to the day before ~~an~~ exam, I would be dancing at an Honours level. I k~~new~~ because Miss De Ville said so. She held my hands ~~and~~ said, "Catherine if you dance like that tomor~~row~~ you'll get Honours."

But I never did and this is why. The night be~~fore~~ an exam, Mom's friend, Pauline, would come ~~over~~ carrying her bag of curlers and spiky hairpins.

A CERTIFICATE SHOWING I COULD DO WELL IN EXAMS IN SPITE OF HAIR CURLERS AND PANIC

After I washed my hair, Pauline went to work. She combed out my hair, ignoring my shrieks as she tore through the knots. Then she wrapped strands of hair around the curlers and pinned them into place with sharp hairpins.

"Ow," I yelled. "Stop sticking them into my head!"

"We can't stop till you look like a hedgehog with curls," she said, winding another hank of hair around a curler and jabbing it into place.

When at last she was finished, she gave me a little bolster with a dent in the middle to use instead of a pillow. My neck rested on the dent and the curlers stuck over the other side. This was supposed to make it easy to sleep. Actually, it was impossible. The night before an exam was spent twisting, turning, and worrying.

But I'm not blaming my poor showing at ballet exams on Pauline. She was doing her best to help me. (Mom and I were hopeless at doing our hair ourselves. She went to the hairdresser's every week, and every Saturday morning, before my ballet lesson, I went over to Sari-next-door to get my hair wound round a special cloth rat - shaped like a doughnut with a hole in

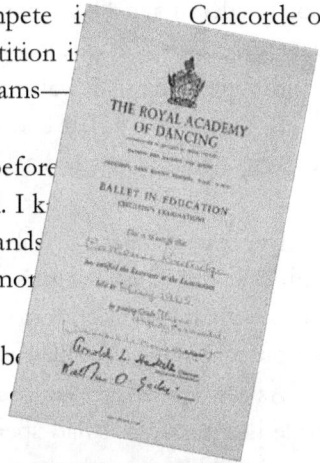

the middle - into a ballerina bun and pinned into place at the nape of my neck.)

In the morning, Mom drove me to the examination hall. Miss De Ville arranged my curls into a beautiful Margot Fonteyn bun at the nape of the neck and sprayed it to within an inch of its life. I changed into my white tunic, pink tights and pink ballet shoes, the special exam kind, with ribbons, not elastics. I felt like a perfect ballerina, ready to amaze and delight the examiner. Miss De Ville gave me a good luck kiss.

But the minute I walked into the examination hall my legs turned to wool, my arms whirled like windmills, and I felt sick with anxiety. Exams always ended in tears and a 'Satisfactory' pass mark. Nothing higher.

**

Every year, Miss De Ville held a Christmas party at the studio. She did not wear her usual trousers and twinset outfit. Instead she put on a pretty dress with a wide skirt, festooned the studio with ribbons and balloons, and set out all kinds of cookies, iced cakes, sweets, chips, and soft drinks.

As we arrived in our best party dresses, we lined up to give Miss De Ville her presents. I had spent hours deciding what to give her and hoped she would like mine the best.

Before we left, Miss De Ville gave each girl a gift.

"Thank you for the beautiful box of soap, Catherine. Here's something for you, Lovey," and she kissed me and handed me a little package. It was funny how she was the only one who called me "Catherine." I loved how my full name sounded when she said it. And she was also the only one who could call me "Lovey" without making me wince and pull faces. When Grampa called me "Lovey," I wanted to tell him not to.

One day, there was lots of excitement and smiles at the studio. Miss De Ville was getting married. She invited all the girls in the studio to her wedding. She was marrying Günter, the German businessman who had an office next door to the ballet studio. She got married in the church near the studio. I wore a purple corduroy tent dress and matching cap, and felt very elegant.

After her marriage, Miss De Ville closed her studio and I moved to one where they taught the Cechetti method, which was more rigorous than Royal Academy.

Ruth, the teacher, was the complete opposite of Miss De Ville. For some reason she took against me. "Cathy, you can go to the back of the class," she said. "I don't need to see you do your *grands jetés* again. They weren't very good the first time and I don't expect they will be any better the next."

I tried not to cry. I knew I was good at ballet. Why couldn't Ruth see that?

But there was one good thing about being at Ruth's. For some reason Mom had a change of heart and allowed me to dance in a show Ruth was putting on with the girls from her studio. I was in the *corps de ballet*. In Act I, I was the day sky in a pale blue costume with toe shoes to match. In Act II, I was part of the night sky, in a beautiful filmy dark blue and black costume with sequins, and there were even sequins on my pointe shoes.

I kept the night sky costume for years after I outgrew it, taking it out of the playroom cupboard every now and then to look at it and wish that it still fitted.

I went *en pointe* when I was 11. This was the great consummation devoutly to be wished for by every girl doing ballet. I was instantly excellent at it, even though my toes were the wrong shape for dancing *en pointe*, too long and uneven. I wished then that I had toes like my mother's, short and even, so they could take the weight of my body without bending under and getting the horrible calluses that the feet of ballet dancers always get. I doused my feet in purple methylated spirits because a book I'd read said this would toughen the toes when you first started dancing *en pointe*.

But my whole family rebelled after the first two or three stinking applications, and my long elegant toes were left to get calloused or blistered or corn-ridden—whatever it turned out to be.

The struggle to find the right teacher and to be allowed to perform in Eisteddfodau and at Concorde, the two major dance competitions of the year, continued for many years. I tried everything, relying heavily on hunger strikes (which usually lasted a day, and were supplemented by secret trips to the biscuit tins in the pantry) and extended sulks, until I went to high school at Roedean.

On the day of the entrance exam my dream of becoming a world famous ballerina came to an abrupt and final end. After the entrance exam there was an interview with the headmistress, the terrifying Mrs. Raikes of myth and legend. When it was my turn to be ushered into the Presence, Mrs. Joan Raikes peered down over the top of her half-moon glasses and spoke in her creaky, yet commanding, English voice. "Catherine, what do you want to be when you grow up?"

"A ballerina, Mrs. Raikes."

"Pah, all you South Africans are crazy about ballet. With your brains you should concentrate on the academic side of things."

And since my parents shared this view, and since the school hours at Roedean were from 7:45 am to 5 pm, *and* there was still homework when you got home, that was the end of becoming a ballerina. There was just no time for it. I gave up my ambition of being accepted at the Royal School of Ballet on Hogarth Road in London. That dream had been fuelled for years by the regular arrival of *The Dancing Times* magazine from England. These magazines were filled with information about auditions and scholarships to the Royal School of Ballet. But by the time the magazines reached Johannesburg, after a sea journey of six weeks, the deadlines for the scholarships and auditions had long passed.

I still didn't give up entirely, though. I created a stage name and practised a flourishing signature for autographing programmes and my worn-out ballet slippers for adoring fans when I became a world-famous ballerina. Because that it was ballerinas did. I had gone backstage once after a performance by a Russian ballerina, and although I was shocked to see how old and haggard she looked close up in her dressing-room, with her hair flattened under its stocking cap, I was still thrilled to get an autographed ballet shoe. My books with their photographs of great ballerinas, with names like Alicia Markova, Galina Ulyanova, Svetlana Beriosova, and my beloved Margot Fonteyn, showed that it was essential to have a Russian or French name if you wanted to become a *prima ballerina assoluta*. Besides, I was in love with Rudolph Nureyev, the great Russian dancer who had defected to the west with a spectacular leap over the barrier at the airport in Montreal when the company was touring Canada. So I chose the name 'Nadia Newmark'.

But that name only ever appeared in signatures in the autograph books of my friends or on the fly-leaf of my ballet books. I was not allowed to use it when I performed. For that I was plain, very English, Catherine Kentridge.

27—PARENTS AT HOME

My mother and I both had long, dark, fine hair. Boys loved the way my hair looked when it was brushed and shiny and falling to midway down my back. But they didn't know about the tears and misery it took to get it like that. The untangling would be a half hour of torture after each hair wash. I cried and whined as I knelt on the hard wooden mat, bending my head over the edge of the bath tub. My mother held the shower in one hand and worked the shampoo into my scalp with the other.

MOM AND DAD'S ENGAGEMENT PHOTO—AUGUST, 1951.

"Ow! Mom, you're hurting me. Stop pulling!"

"Stop crying or you can do it yourself."

"The water's too hot, and my eyes are stinging."

She rinsed my hair one last time and poured beer over it. I closed my eyes and mouth very tight. When my hair dried, it was sticky and smelt bad, but it shone. Sometimes she used vinegar instead, to get out all the soap and to make my hair shine. This didn't smell too good, either. But the most unpleasant smell was the ammonia that we used for washing the hairbrushes.

For years, Mom wore her hair in a bun. You could tell where she'd been by the trail of hairpins that were always falling out. She went to the hairdresser once a week to get her hair done, emerging with a very stiff lacquered do. As a special treat, once or twice a year she took me to Rosebank where her hairdresser, Mario, had his salon. He would keep me waiting for hours after the appointed time. Then just when I was sure my turn had finally come to go to the basin and begin the beauty process, I

MOM ON HER WEDDNG DAY, JANUARY 15, 1952, WITH HER MOTHER-IN-LAW, MAY KENTRIDGE, AND HER MOTHER, IRENE GEFFEN.

would be shunted aside for yet another hour while a more important, grownup, regular, client had her hair washed and curled. When Mario finally finished with me, I gazed into the mirror and hated how I looked. I was not like Cathy at all, my hair all stiff, teased, and glued into place with hairspray. How could my mother bear to go through this every single week?

What I loved were the rare times when my mother sat on the sofa in the living room and I stretched out with my head on her lap and she stroked my hair while we talked. Sometimes we laughed about quite grown-up things and there were confessions.

"Dad likes to stroke my hair, but he always messes it up. So he is not allowed to after I've just been to the hairdresser," she said.

"Perhaps it's because he doesn't have that much of his own left," I said, and we laughed.

**

"Dad, can we have some more of *Great Expectations*? Please, please, just one more chapter tonight?"

Dad sat on the edge of the bed and began.

"'Hold your noise!' cried a terrible voice."

I shrieked and grabbed my mother's hand tightly. I preferred it when he read Jane Austen to us.

"'It is a truth universally acknowledged that a single man in possession of a good fortune must be in want of a wife.'"

Dad liked to tease us by seeming very reluctant to read "just one more chapter." But we knew he really enjoyed reading to us and being cajoled, and we were never disappointed.

One night he was reading *Wuthering Heights*. The story was becoming more and more exciting. I held my breath. Heathcliff opened the window and called out into the storm, "Cathy, come back, my beloved Cathy, come back!"

I burst into tears. It was too much that his lost love had the same name as mine.

But nothing was as terrifying to my waking and dreaming imagination as the Black Riders in *The Lord of the Rings*. I became so scared that my father had to stop reading. I was sure they were after me. A few months later we were driving through a lonely stretch of veld, in the dead of night. Bushfires blazed on either side of the road. William and I were tucked cozily into the back seat of the car, me stretched across Ellen's lap and William on a makeshift bed of suitcases and blankets at her feet. I was almost asleep when a terrible thought struck me.

"Daddy, Mommy, help! The Black Riders are coming for us!"

It was shortly after this that Dad switched to reading aloud P.G. Wodehouse novels in which nothing frightening ever happened. The challenge was to get through a whole page of Bertie Wooster's idiocy without bursting out laughing. We howled at his antics as he tried in vain to outwit Jeeves, who would not allow "sir" to get his own way about that loud tie or pink silk shirt he was determined to wear to dinner with his Aunt Dahlia.

But it was not so funny watching my parents decide about dresses and suits and ties for their dinner parties. For some reason, my mother and father always got very irritable before a dinner party. They would be upstairs in their bedroom putting on evening clothes; my mother opening and closing drawers of jewellery and choosing which lipstick to wear, me hovering.

If I asked a question or tried to chat to my parents, they gave short, snappish answers. Why did they have dinner parties if it made them so cross?

Mom took much longer to get ready than Dad. While she was putting the finishing touches to her hair and makeup, Dad had long since put on his dinner jacket, black bowtie and the velvet slippers with the embroidered foxes. Then he went downstairs to the backroom to check the bottles of wine and spirits. Were they exactly the kind and the number he had ordered?

"Cathy, have you checked off all the wines?"

It was my job to do the first count of the bottles in the boxes that the

MOM (FELICIA KENTRIDGE) AND DAD (SYDNEY KENTRIDGE) ON THEIR WEDDING DAY, JANUARY 15, 1952.

men from Solly Kramers Wines and Spirits had delivered. I had to compare the contents of the boxes with the invoice. And I had to count the wine glasses which were supplied by the liquor store.

William and I loved waiting for the first guest to ring the front doorbell. This signalled the start of the dinner party. The guests arrived in their best evening clothes, and we showed them into the living room.

"Mom, Ulla and Chris are here!" I yelled.

My mother hurried downstairs, her jewellery sparkling and her face smiling a greeting. My father offered the guests drinks. Joseph, in white jacket and dark trousers, handed round a tray of savoury hors d'oeuvres: spicy cheese biscuits, smoked *snoek* and mayonnaise on crackers, asparagus and cheese on little rolls. Sometimes William and I were allowed to offer the tray to the guests. And no one minded if we paid ourselves with a snack or three.

At a signal from Ellen, which I conveyed to my mother in a whisper, the grown-ups went in to dinner and William and I ran into the kitchen. Ellen said we could taste some of the dishes before they were sent in to the dining room. We had long since had our own supper. I liked the lamb stew, but let William taste the magenta beetroot soup with its circle of cream sprinkled with chives. We fought over who would get more of the pieces Ellen had trimmed from the thin layers of the hazelnut meringue and coffee cream, which the guests would be getting for pudding.

From where we sat, we could hear gusts of laughter or snippets of conversation coming from the dining room, the scraping of a fork on a plate, glasses clinking together for a toast. Between courses, Mom or Dad rang a little silver bell to let the servants in the kitchen know that it was time to bring on or remove the dishes.

After dinner, the ladies would go upstairs to Mom's bedroom to powder their noses and squirt French perfume onto their throats and wrists. In the dining room, the men drank more wine and smoked. Then the ladies

GROUP PHOTO AT MOM AND DAD'S WEDDING. LEFT TO RIGHT: BERYL MORTON, ZOE GIRLING (MY AUNT ZOE, MOM'S SISTER WHO WENT TO CANADA), ARNOLD KENTRIDGE (WHO GAVE ME THE PIANO BEFORE HE LEFT FOR ENGLAND), DAD, MOM, MORRIS KENTRIDGE, IRENE GEFFEN, MAX GEFFEN.

rejoined the men in the sitting room for coffee, cake, chocolate and liqueurs.

Next day, the sitting room smelled of stale tobacco and eight different kinds of perfume. If we were lucky, there might be cake or dessert left over and Ellen would put some in our lunch boxes for school.

**

Every year, my parents threw a New Year's Eve Party. They would invite 30 or 40 friends to dinner and dancing at Number 72. Sometimes Dad hired a band to dance to and rented a wooden dance floor which was laid over the brick patio. He hired Dante, a very popular and famous Italian bartender, to serve drinks and supervise a troop of waiters. Ellen was very busy in the kitchen preparing wonderful food. When William and I were a bit older, we were each allowed to invite a friend or two.

The drinks table was set up on the vine-roofed porch outside the sitting room. The bartenders served me glass after glass of red fizzy lemonade and Fanta Orange.

At midnight, there was an uproar from the streets below, with people banging on the lamp-posts and shouting "Happy! Happy!"

**

For many years Mom's clothes were custom-made by Mrs. Noble, who lived in Orange Grove, the Italian part of Johannesburg. The house itself felt Italian from the moment you saw it, with its pillared verandah and neat straight path from the gate to the front steps. Crucifixes and images of Christ with a bleeding heart, and of the Virgin Mary, hung on the walls of her tiled entrance hall. The fitting room, with its swathes of wonderful fabrics, silks, satins, lace, brocades, and velvets, was like walking into a rainbow. You had to watch out for the pins, though. They were everywhere. She had books of the latest fashions from Rome and Paris. Mom, Mrs. Noble, and I pored over these glossy magazines, taking hours to decide what dress or jacket or skirt my mother would like and which fabric to use.

MOM, CIRCA 1965

"Oh, Mom, you would look so lovely in that pink chiffon dress. I'm sure Mrs. Noble could make it for you."

When my mother had made her choice and it was time for a fitting, Mrs. Noble, her mouth full of pins, fussed round her. Mom stood on a box and turned slowly in a circle while Mrs. Noble, on her knees, adjusted the hem, spraying white chalk onto the material to mark the correct length. Weeks later, when the dress was ready, Mom looked like one of the photographs in the fashion magazines.

**

I spent many evenings feeling anxious about my parents' safety and well-being, especially when they were out at night, which was often. Sometimes, if they were late returning from a dinner party or the theatre I got into a panic, convinced they had been in a traffic accident. I wanted to telephone the Flying Squad. I had total faith that if I dialled 999, the squad would rush off in their flying cars, with wings and wheels, to find my parents and bring them safely home in an instant. But Mom and Dad always arrived back the minute before I had finally plucked up courage to dial. I only just had time to dive under the covers before their quiet voices whispered goodnight to Ellen, who had babysat us while they were out. They came softly into my bedroom, and I was enveloped in my mother's perfume when she leaned down to kiss me.

28—PARENTS AT WORK

Both my parents worked. This was yet another difference between me and most of the other girls at my school. Not only was I Jewish, but my mother actually worked. Other mothers played bridge or tennis, got their hair done, or shopped all day. They never had to do any housework because they all had servants to do it for them. So did my mother. But she had a career. Like my father, she was a lawyer, an advocate.

I didn't know what kind of law she practised. But I knew it was hard for her to be a mother and to be an advocate at the same time. She was always tired. She went to her Chambers with Dad. They were in the same building, Innes Chambers, in the heart of town, across from the court, but on different floors. All the other advocates in Johannesburg had chambers in the same building.

Mom also worked with an organization called the Black Sash, white women who wore black sashes over their dresses and protested about the way non-whites were treated. I knew that it was very important work. I also knew it was very dangerous to protest, and they risked being attacked by policemen and their vicious Alsatian dogs, or by anybody else who didn't agree with what they were doing. They might even be put into a Black Maria and taken off to prison. I was very afraid that might happen to Mom.

Usually, Mom worked in the morning and came home in the afternoon. I loved it when she fetched me from school. The grey car with its red stripe seemed to smile as it came into sight around the bend of the road. I tried not to mind when I heard the girls standing waiting for their mother or their chauffeur to fetch them, saying loudly, "Cathy, your mother's so pretty. What happened to *you*?"

But there was something about my mother's work that made me very cross. My mother's work meant she had to think about lots of other things besides family, and couldn't know exactly when her work would finish and she could come home. She couldn't fetch me from school every day or do things with me whenever I wanted her to and spoil me like my other friends' mothers spoiled their daughters, and sometimes I felt hard done by. Sometimes I would come home from school, having got a lift from a friend's mother or taken the bus. I would have struggled up the steep drive carrying my heavy sack of books, and there would be Mom, sitting in the study having a cup of tea and a biscuit.

"Why didn't you fetch me?" I said, throwing down my sack, the brown canvas bag in which all girls from Roedean carried their books.

"I'd already arranged with Sandra's mother to fetch you." Or "I didn't know I'd be home in time."

"But you know I don't like Sandra and she doesn't like me, and her mother always asks me what marks I got in my test today and it's very embarrassing."

If I'd actually had to take the bus, I would be even crosser:

"But Mom, I had to wait for ages for the bus and the drive is so steep and my sack is so heavy."

Mom just gave me a look. Then she put on her glasses and shut the door to the study and I knew enough to keep away and not disturb her till Ellen told me it was time to call her for supper.

We knew Dad worked on a lot of cases to do with politics. Names were spoken in hushed voices—Bram Fischer and Albert Luthuli. They were banned or on the run and we had to be very careful not to be overheard when we said their names or we could get into big trouble. We knew our phones might be tapped and that we had to take particular care not to mention anything we had heard our parents saying if a stranger on the phone began asking us questions.

My father had consultations at the house in his study on weekends when he was in the middle of a big trial. Other advocates and attorneys involved in the case bumped up the drive in their sleek cars, cursing with every jolt. They went through a side door into the study, or into the dining room if there were too many of them to fit into the study.

William and I kept well away, playing in other parts of the house. If the lawyers were there in the afternoon, Ellen baked a cake or biscuits and I was allowed to carry in the tea tray, first knocking on the glass door for permission to come in.

Often, when there was no one about, I went into the study and looked at some of the legal documents. There were briefs tied with ribbons, some red and some green. The paper was grey-blue. The documents had the name "Adv. Sydney Kentridge, S.C., 621 Innes Chambers" on them. I saw words like *sine die*, which Dad said was pronounced "signy die," or *Plaintiff,* or *Defendant, alleged that* or *decree nisi* or *damages*. Sometimes I came across detailed descriptions of the horrible things people had done to each other, or what had happened in a car crash. Often pages were filled with sentences full of long, dull words— "the said appellant," "the aforementioned," or "Notwithstanding heretofore." I knew I was not supposed to be reading any of this. I jumped at every noise, thinking my father had found me out and would be very angry.

Other times I would open the daily papers, the *Rand Daily Mail* or *The Star,* and see Dad's name and photograph because he was involved in a case about a political prisoner, or the editor of a national newspaper, or a major company. It made me very proud to open the paper and see his name there with a photograph of him standing outside the Supreme Court in his advocate's jacket and white tabs and dark trousers. So wah to Caroline, a girl in my ballet class who was very plump and wore glasses and boasted that her father was better than mine because he was a "barrister, and yours is only an advocate." Anyway, I was far better at ballet than she was.

As a special treat during school holidays, or if a birthday was coming up or we were going away and needed to get foreign money from the bank downstairs, I would come to Dad's Chambers. Mom drove us in to town and we parked underground beneath Innes Chambers. Then we took the lift to the sixth floor.

I couldn't walk straight in to see him. First the lady at the front desk had to check if he was busy. If so, I had to wait. Then I would be shown into the anteroom where his secretary, Miss Shulamit Hanson, with her glasses and beehive hair, sat typing.

Through a half-open door across the corridor I could see the office manager, Mr. Kronson, sitting at his desk doing nothing in particular. He had been there so long, he was like part of the furniture.

The windows of Dad's office faced the court across the street. The room was lined with bookshelves from floor to ceiling, filled with law reports and volumes of legislation. On a high shelf were some pottery figures of advocates in wigs and navy-blue gowns and glasses perched on the edge of their noses. There was a painting of the head of a medieval woman, not quite looking straight at you, wearing a pointed hat with a veil floating from its pointed end. Her expression was very calm.

If it were lunchtime, Dad would take me to Chez André, a French restaurant that all the advocates frequented, till the day André refused to serve lunch to a black American diplomat. After that, some of the advocated refused to go to Chez André again.

If it was my birthday, Dad would come downstairs to Lilliputs, the toy shop, with me, and I would walk round the shop fingering the things I wanted, and being very sad when I saw how expensive they were. Then we would go back upstairs and I would sit quietly in Dad's Chambers or in the waiting room till he had finished gathering all the papers he needed to take home with him and had put them into his brown leather briefcase.

Sometimes it would turn out that he had gone back to Lilliputs and bought me one of the toys I coveted.

Then we'd go down to the car in the basement under the Chambers and drive home through the evening rush hour.

The wonderful thing was that although Dad worked every day, from early in the morning till just before supper and then again for many hours after supper, and most Saturdays and Sundays as well, he always seemed to have time to help me and William with homework if we asked. He was best with Latin and history and English and he didn't get impatient with us.

After a while, he would say, "Darling, I hope you understand about Napoleon's strategy now. I'm afraid I have to go back to the study to work on a case."

That was the signal to finish the homework on my own, so I would shine in class next day when the history teacher asked me a question about Napoleon's Russian Campaign.

29—BROTHERS AND SISTERS

I was the eldest child. But at first, I was only older than one other child, my brother William, who was exactly 18 months younger, and very much sweeter. I was born to be a bossy older sister. William was almost invariably good-natured. But when he did get angry, watch out – he could be vicious, or even worse, he would start to laugh the angrier I got, till I would have

hysterics, laughing and crying. The more hysterical I became the more he laughed, so it was no use telling on him.

But he was also the one who took the job of protecting his big sister very seriously. One day when I was about five and he was about three,

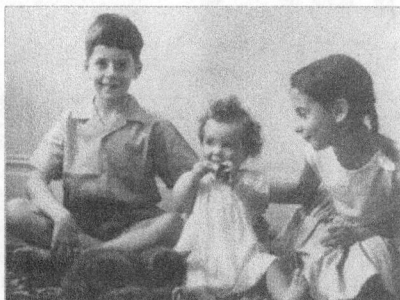

WILLIAM, ELIZA, THE MOST BEAUTIFUL LITTLE SISTER IN THE WORLD, AND CATHY.

Mom took me to a grown-up hairdresser. William came with us. The hairdresser made me weep and scream in pain as she pulled and tugged at my scalp to get the knots out of my long, very fine hair. All of a sudden, William rushed up and kicked the hairdresser hard in the shins.

"That's for making my sister cry!"

**

William sucked his thumb. He sucked it so much that I was afraid he would suck it down to nothing, the way you sucked a hard-boiled sweet. It started off big and got smaller and smaller and then just vanished.

"William, stop sucking your thumb!" yelled Mom.

"William, your thumb will disappear and then you'll be sorry!" I yelled.

He went on sucking.

My aunt Zoë tried to bribe him. When our parents were overseas and we were staying at Zoë's, she began her scheme to cure William of thumb sucking.

Every day, when she came back from work, she would ask William if he had sucked his thumb that day. If the answer was no, he got a little present. If the answer was yes, he still got a little present, even though I protested; and sometimes I would tell Zoë the truth.

"Zoë, he sucked his thumb today, I saw him. He shouldn't get a present. It's not fair."

But he got a present all the same.

He did stop sucking his thumb before it could disappear completely. But, by that time, I was sure it was a lot smaller and had a completely different shape than the thumb he didn't suck.

But William didn't tell on me and Oliver when we crawled under Zoë's bed one day, clutching a packet of cigarettes. We saw Zoë and Harry smoking all day, so I said, "Why don't we try smoking to see what it's like?"

MATHEW AND ELIZA, ABOUT THREE AND FIVE

Oliver took two cigarettes out of the packet. I put one in my mouth and he put one in his. We didn't try to light them. That would really have been asking for trouble. We just sucked on them.

"Ugh! It's disgusting!" we said, after half a minute and spat them out, and rushed out from under the bed to brush our teeth and drink lots of granadilla juice to get the horrible taste out of our mouths.

William was a whiz at Meccano, building complex engines operated with methylated spirits. And as for board games, the situation was hopeless. I was simply unable to win a game of Monopoly, Diplomacy, or Scrabble against William. Sometimes the Monopoly tournament might go on for a whole weekend, reluctantly abandoned at bed time and enthusiastically resumed after breakfast. I couldn't even beat him at Canasta.

From time to time, William enjoyed making me really angry. One day I found him going through my cupboards where I kept my most personal supplies, including bras and sanitary towels.

"Get out of there! How DARE you! I'm telling!"

William began to laugh.

"It's not funny. How would you like it if I went through YOUR things?"

He laughed louder.

I stomped off to find Mom, William trailing behind me, laughing more loudly, till I was laughing too, and crying and shouting.

By the time we found Mom, I couldn't get the words out to tell her what William had been doing.

William became a devastating croquet player in the Sunday tournaments he held with his friends on the front lawn. The shouts of triumph and despair floated up to my open window as I sat swotting for Matric in the November and December heat, listening to LM radio, with its incomprehensible Portuguese time signals on the hour. The South African government had banned the Beatles for claiming they were "greater then God," so we couldn't listen to them on SABC radio. But Portuguese East Africa was not governed by South African law, so any time you wanted a fix of Beatles, you tuned in to LM radio.

There were only three things in the world that I was better at than William—singing, dancing, and playing the piano. William didn't even try to dance. He knew there was no point. Nor did he try to learn the piano, but had clarinet lessons instead, practising for hours with loud, unmusical squawks in front of the mirror in his bedroom. The family had many opportunities to judge whose singing was better—or worse. At least once a week, at bedtime, I would ask William to sing "There is a tavern in the town, in the town," a song he'd been taught at school. He would begin to bellow and I would take up the song. Our bedrooms were across the hall from each other, so we had to sing very loudly to hear each other. The family would be treated to a raucous and unharmonious duet for all five or six verses of the song. Over our heads, on the roof, the pigeons stomped up and down as if dancing in iron boots to our singing.

But William was the one who was by far the best at art. Mom and Dad framed the splash painting he did when he was six, and which somehow looked so much better than my splash painting, also framed, so I wouldn't feel hurt.

At Nina Campbell-Quine's Saturday morning art classes, William was the undisputed star, with Clare Gavron as a close second. Nina's art classes were held at her beautiful, exotic house in a suburb of Johannesburg. There you learned about drawing with charcoal, pastel crayons, watercolours and Khoki pens. Nina wafted through the many rooms of her studio, dressed in a kaftan, her plain, round white face crowned by an elaborate hairstyle. The hairstyle was quite spectacular, the hair scraped back from her face and wound through chunky glass-gem encrusted papier-mâché bracelets she had made. She had a black satin eyepatch over one eye. She wore embroidered Turkish slippers with turned-up toes. We all adored her husband Billy with his white hair, and his old pale green British sports car.

Nina was vague when it came to teaching.

She stood over me and said, "This line needs to be little more…" or "You might want to do …" and let her voice trail off, never quite finishing the sentence. I was always left wondering what exactly Nina meant and how I could make my charcoal sketch or watercolour look even the least bit like the object I was supposed to be drawing. It took me years to realize that a 'still life' was an arrangement of objects like flowers, fruit, and vases, and did not mean a portrait of someone sitting very still.

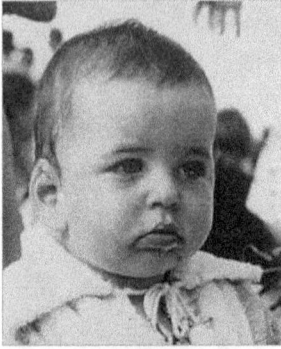

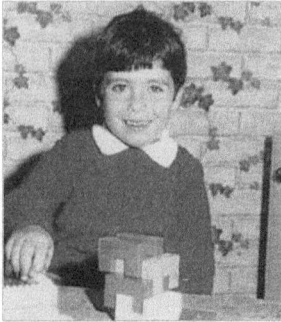

WILLIAM AS A BABY—HE WAS ALWAYS THE SWEETEST, AND MATTHEW, A VERY SWEET LITTLE BROTHER, AGED ABOUT THREE.

At the annual party and art exhibition at the studio, my friend Andrea and I played our guitars and sang for the guests; songs like *Blowing in the Wind* and *Sipping Spiders Through a Straw*. Each student had at least one example of work on display, and the stars such as William and Clare had several, and there were works of art that Nina herself had made.

Once or twice a year, Nina and Billy invited friends, pupils, and their parents to an evening of slides at their house, which was attached to the studio. Nina and Billy travelled all over the world and took photographs that were art in themselves. They told stories about the places they had been to and served delicious things to eat.

**

I was eight and a half when my sister Eliza was born. Immediately and ever after I knew that Eliza was the sweetest and prettiest little sister anyone could ever have. When the baby came home from the Marymount, the nursing home where I, William, Eliza, and Matthew were born, I appointed myself Eliza's nurse and guardian. At the slightest murmur from her, I rushed into her room to pick her up, rock, soothe or sing to her, or walk her pram up and down the room till she settled again. Eliza had many pairs of booties in white or pink or pale blue, lovingly and painstakingly knitted by her big sister, whose *pièce de résistance* for the baby was a blue bonnet that buttoned under the chin. In the morning when she woke, I brought her into Mom and Dad's bedroom so Mom could feed her.

I crawled round Eliza's pram chanting, "Chinese men, Chinese women" over and over, making her laugh and laugh. And I was the one who saw Eliza take her first steps and shrieked so loudly with excitement that my mother and the servants came running, worried something dreadful had happened.

One day, something dreadful did happen. I was at school, in Afrikaans with Mevrou, when a message came

WILLIAM WITH HIS LITTLE SISTER, ELIZA, AND BABY BROTHER, MATTHEW.

for me to go to Mrs. Gilham's office. I wondered what trouble I had got into this time. But when I arrived trembling in her office, Mrs. Gilham said, "Your father has just phoned me to tell me your little sister has broken her arm. She rolled off the table while having her nappy changed."

My heart stopped and I burst into tears.

**

With Matthew, who arrived a couple of years later, I was not at all enthralled. I thought my parents should have stopped at Eliza and told them so quite plainly. And besides, if the baby boy was to be admitted into the family, his name should be Toby, not Matthew. But those in favour of Matthew argued that if you called "Toby!" all the neighbourhood dogs would come running.

By Matthew's arrival, I was an expert on babies. I knew when their crying meant something was wrong and when it was just an exercising of the lungs. So I did not dance attendance on him. In fact, I barely tolerated him. It didn't help that when we moved house and he came home from the nursing home, Eliza turned from being a perfect baby who slept all night, to one who woke up crying several times every night. I blamed it all on Matthew. He had messed up the family.

When he was about four, Matthew made a new friend, a little Greek boy called Pio, who lived just down the road from Number 72. One day Matthew and Pio sat on the top step of the stairs, just outside Mom and Dad's bedroom.

"Fuck!" said Pio, quietly.

"Fuck!" said Matthew, quietly. I wasn't sure that I had heard what I thought I'd heard.

"Fuck!" said Pio more loudly. "Fuck!" even louder.

"Fuck!" said Matthew more loudly. "Fuck!" said Matthew, even louder.

"Don't you dare say that! Where did you learn that word?" I yelled. They said it again louder, more yells from me, and then Ellen heard them and said, "Matthew and Pio, those are not nice words. You must not say them."

Next time when Pio came to visit and they started up with their, "Fuck!", I followed Mom's advice and did not respond at all, just smiled and walked past them as they sat on the stairs. The fun went out of saying that word. Nobody was reacting, so Matthew and Pio went back to chasing each other up and down the stairs.

When Eliza and Matthew were a little older, they shared the porch, the upstairs room adjoining mine, which had been converted into a bedroom from a glassed-in porch. The doorway between my bedroom and theirs gave daily opportunities for "the children," as I called them when I was being polite, to rush through my bedroom laughing and chattering, at very early hours of the morning.

And then for a few weeks, I had to share their bedroom while mine was being renovated. I could not sleep at all during that time. Matthew had inherited the curse of the male Kentridges–he snored so loudly, it was a wonder he didn't wake himself up.-Long after William and I were eating all our meals with the grownups in the dining room, Eliza and Matthew were still *the children* and ate early in the kitchen.

30—SERVANTS

Ellen, our cook, and Eggy, the nanny for Matthew and Eliza, cowered behind the door in the passage leading to the kitchen. Someone was knocking loudly at the front door.

"Miss Cathy, please see who it is," said Ellen.

"Why don't you go? It's not my job to open the front door," I said.

"But it might be the Pass Inspector, and I am afraid my papers are not in order," said Eggy.

"I am afraid, too," said Ellen. "He could send me away from here back to Thaba'nchu, and then Bosky would starve, and I would never see you again."

"Last time he wanted to throw me in jail because I had not renewed my Pass," said Eggy.

Servants always dreaded the knock at the door of the Pass Inspector, coming to check that their Pass Books were in order. And a Pass Inspector could stop any non-European at any time anywhere and demand to see their Pass. The Pass Books gave black people permission to work in the white city of Johannesburg and to be living in a white suburb.

I opened the door, ready to say brave and angry words to the Pass Inspector. But it was only a delivery man.

"Don't you know you're supposed to go to the back door?" I said.

Delivery men always went to the back door.

I grew up with servants. There were nannies, a cook, an ironing lady, a housemaid, a houseboy, and a gardener. Some were full-time and lived on the property; others came in three or four times a week to work. Ellen, Lydia, and John were the live-in servants at Number 2 St. John's Road—Stonecrest.

Whenever I was unhappy or angry, Ellen was the one I turned to for comfort or to calm me down. And she knew so many stories about what

William and I had got up to when we were little. She would talk about the time I had been rude to my grandmother May and made her so angry that she sent me to Coventry for three weeks, or William kicking the hairdresser. She would also sing, in her sweet voice, a lullaby or a popular song. Often I did not know what the words were or what they meant. I loved it when she sang to me. "I was dancing with my darling to the Ternity Waltz," or "Mangwane pulleleh ginne lucky poolah – please open the door it is raining outside, find me a girl and I'll make her your bride." Sometimes she would tell us about Bosky.

Bosky was her son and was about my age. He lived far away in Thaba'nchu, in the Orange Free State, looked after by his grandparents and aunts, while Ellen looked after us in Johannesburg. Once a year on her annual holiday she went home to Thaba'nchu to see Bosky. He almost never came to visit her at the house on St. John's Road, nor later at the house on Houghton Drive.

ERNEST, EGGY, JOSEPH, ELLEN, CATHY, WILLIAM AND HIS WIFE, ANNE STANWIX, AND ELIZA (1983)

Ellen taught me manners. She didn't like the way I slurped my tea, which I drank piping hot and black. "Miss Cathy, you mustn't drink your tea like that. You sound like the Farmer's Wife!" she said.

When I crunched my toast too noisily, she said, "You sound like mice in the bread tin."

Apart from looking after us all, Ellen was the cook, the baker, and the protector of my mother's housekeeping budget and supplies.

In our house there were weekly rations of white bread, sugar, and mielie-meal for the servants, and general groceries for the rest of the household. Every Monday morning, my mother phoned Spar Grocers in Orange Grove to place an order. The groceries were delivered that afternoon. Next day, Mom doled them out so that each servant got exactly the same amount. All the other groceries were carefully locked away in the pantry cupboards,

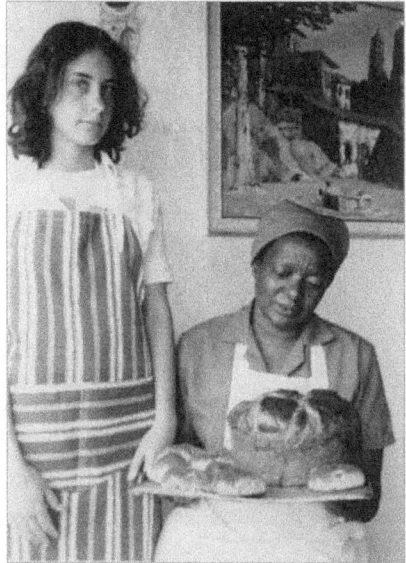

ELIZA AND ELLEN WITH FRESHLY BAKED BREAD AND SWEET BUNS

especially if the order contained Zoo Biscuits, the ones with hard white icing decorated with animal shapes in bright reds and blues and greens, or the Romany Creams with coconut and chocolate. Any chance we got, William and I raided the cupboard for our favourites.

As soon as the grocery man in his tiny van had shuddered up and down the stone drive with its hairpin bend, and the groceries had been shared out and packed away, the trouble would begin.

Ellen kept jealous guard over the pantry cupboards, and would report to me on anything missing. Eggy, whose real name was Ecclesia, was the other nanny. She and Ellen did not get on. They took turns to take me aside.

"That one, she is taking food from the pantry cupboard. I saw her taking the sugar," said Ellen, pointing at Eggy.

"Miss Cathy, you think Ellen is your friend. But she is stealing biscuits; you know I'm telling the truth," said Eggy.

My mother was always addressed as "Madam" and my father as "Master."

"Miss Cathy, please go and ask the Madam what she wants me to cook for dinner?"

"The Master is not home yet, sir. He will be here by six o'clock," said Ellen, answering the phone.

131

Almost all the Masters and Madams, the white South Africans who had servants, referred to the women as "girls," and to the men as "boys," regardless of age and no matter whether the "Madam" or the "Master" was older or younger than the servant. Sometimes, if the employers wished to be more polite, they referred to their women servants as "maids."

"What a nuisance!" one Madam would exclaim to her friend over an afternoon of bridge and bitching, where complaining about your servants was a favourite topic.

"My girl had the day off the other day, just when I was needing her to look after the kids while I went to get my hair done."

"My girl Doris is so lazy; she works only 10 hours a day and now she is asking me for two days off a week! Who does she think she is?"

"You know Phineas, our garden boy? I never trusted him. I always thought he smoked dagga, and the other day, true's God, I caught the stink of it when he came in from the garden with the flowers. I told my husband, No Man, it's time to give Phineas the sack! Let him smoke dagga at his own place!"

"Yes," her friend would say, puffing on her cigarette, or popping a sweet into her mouth from the dish on the table. "What can you expect of them? They don't know any better and they never will!"

And a fourth would add, "My girl is so stupid she made tea with cold water... but you know what *they're* like!"

My parents never referred to their servants as "the girl" or "the boy." And Mom never spoke of her servants in the way the bridge-playing women did. She did not even go to the afternoons of bridge. Unlike those women, Mom worked. She was an advocate.

**

Women servants wore uniforms of pink or blue or green overall dresses that buttoned down the front, starched white aprons with bibs, and headscarves or *doeks* to match. We never saw a woman servant's hair. It was always completely concealed by the doek. On days off, they would wear a smart outfit with a matching all-concealing doek. We almost felt we were seeing her naked if we ever saw a woman servant without her doek. Men servants wore khaki shirts and shorts or long trousers. If they were serving dinner or lunch, they wore a white jacket and dark trousers and highly-polished shoes.

If the servants belonged to a religious sect, they wore its badge at all times, pinned to the front of their uniform. Ellen and Eggy both wore the green felt cloth with the tin star of the ZCC, the Zion Christian Church. Once or twice a year, Ellen and Eggy went with thousands of other ZCC people to Petersburg, in a distant part of the Transvaal, a long and difficult journey, needing many different kinds of transport, to a big meeting of the ZCC. The way they spoke of it, Petersburg was almost as holy as Bethlehem.

JOSEPH, THE GARDENER, PRUNING THE FLOWERS OUTSIDE THE STUDY WINDOW AT 72 HOUGHTON DRIVE.

The women and the men servants slept each in his or her own small dark room in the concrete yard at the back of the house. Each room had a narrow iron bedstead, whose legs balanced on bricks standing in tins. This was to keep away *tokoloshes*, evil spirits who would attack you in the middle of the night if your bed were too close to the ground.

Sometimes as a great treat and mark of friendship, Ellen invited me into her room. The air was stuffy as the windows and door were kept tightly closed and locked when Ellen was in the house. On the bed was a hand-embroidered pillowcase with an elaborate design of flowers, and there was an embroidered cloth to cover the small table. Ellen's clothes hung on wire hangers behind the door and her most precious possessions were in a battered suitcase under the bed. The walls had photos of Bosky and of Ellen as a young woman, when she was *much* thinner. The table held a radio and some knickknacks I had given Ellen over the years.

At Number 2 the servants' bathroom doubled as the laundry room At Number 72, they had their own bathroom. A few of the girls I knew did not have special bathrooms for their servants. Their servants had a shower suspended over the outside lavatory. Servants were not allowed to use the inside lavatories or bathrooms, which were strictly for the white families and their friends.

The servants cooked their food in the main kitchen, before or long after they had finished preparing and cleaning up food for the whites. The rancid stench of the cheap meat that employers bought for their servants – usually offal of various sorts—choked your breath as the innards simmered and boiled.

From time to time, Madam would give her cast-off clothes, or Master's, or the children's, to the servants and their children. At Christmas, the presents for the women always included a new dress and, perhaps, a piece of jewellery, as well as money, and new clothes for their children. The men just got money and new clothes for their children.

I never learned any useful words in Sesotho, which was Ellen's native language. But a gardener once taught me some swear words. I trotted these out proudly at every opportunity. It was worth it just for the reactions.

"Eikona, Miss Cathy. Don't say those words."

"What have I said? Why are you looking at me like that?"

But they would look down at the ground and absolutely refuse to tell me what the words meant. So I never found out.

31—WILLIAM'S SCHOOLS

William's schools, King Edward VII Preparatory School (KEPS) and King Edward VII High School (KES) were very different from mine. For one thing, they were all-boys' schools. For another, they were both in walking distance of our house.

And at King Edward's, your academic position in class really mattered. The teachers would decide at the end of each term who came first, second and third, and so on down to the dunces. It was a matter of deep discussion around the table at home, and of great rivalry among the top boys in each class.

My schools never officially bothered about such things, although exam results were always read out

CATHY AT AROUND 13, AS SHE LOOKED WHEN HER FIRST BOYFRIEND, FROM KES, WITH THE BIG HANDSOME NOSE CAME VISITING

from lowest to highest, so we had a good idea of who was best at what subject, as we listened with dread and anticipation to hear our names.

In William's classes, from Grade One to Matric, he was always among the top three. And it was the same two friends who alternated with him for first, second, and third.

William's teachers were all eccentric, some even seemed deranged from what he told us about them. I felt I knew them almost as well as if I had been in their classes, because every evening over supper William would bring the family up to date with the latest craziness. His accent and gestures conjured the teachers to life over the chops and chips.

"You know Miss Smiley? Today she made Bloch cry because she teased him about his name. She never cracks a smile, you know," he said. (That was something else about KEPS and KES. The boys always referred to each other by their surnames.)

His teachers seemed to have much more interesting names than ours. One of the teachers at KEPS was known as Rhino. He had been at KEPS long enough that he had taught Dad, and now he was teaching William.

But it was from high school, at KES, where the staff included The Blob and an Italian woman who taught Latin, that the best stories emerged.

Every evening we waited in breathless anticipation to hear the latest installment. We were almost never disappointed.

"You'll never believe what the Blob did today," said William.

"What, what?" we said.

"You know Meyers who always sits in the back row? Well today, The Blob told him to hold his ruler up in the air. Then he fired at it with an airgun."

There was a stunned silence around the table.

The Blob was responsible for a saying that immediately became one of our family sayings. Sometimes, in the middle of class he would say, "Boys! We are going to begin work on page 96, BUT, *eers… Lav toe!*"

WILLIAM IN HIS KEPS (KING EDWARD PREPARATORY SCHOOL) UNIFORM

Ever after, every time anyone needed to go to the lavatory, especially if it were just before we set out for a trip, they would say, "I have to go *eers*."

Signora, the Latin teacher, taught the boys a most beautiful Italian accent for their Latin. "Boys, you have to keep the verb strictly under control," she said. "If you do not, you will all fail 'oplessly.'"

At KES all the boys had to join cadets, to prepare them for going into the army right after they finished Matric. Being in cadets seemed to involve several things: getting yelled at by the master in charge, wearing a uniform, polishing the huge black boots that went with the uniform, polishing with whiting any part of the uniform that had white in it (such as the belt), and polishing the buckle of your belt till you could see your face in it.

The nearest thing to this that we had at my school was sports with our games teacher. If it were winter, she yelled at us and blasted on her whistle while we ran round and round the hockey pitch. In summer, she perched on the edge of the pool in her short gym skirt, her whistle in her mouth, and blew blasts as we churned up and down the cold pool doing length after length of crawl, backstroke and breast-stroke. I thought she would have done very well as a drill-sergeant in charge of the cadets.

KES had two things of which I was very envious. One of them was a drama club, whose plays I attended whenever William was performing in them. At one I developed a huge 'pash' for a handsome boy called John, who as well as being an actor and having leading roles in the school play also wrote poetry. His poems often featured in the school's magazine, as did William's. Each time William brought home a new issue of the magazine, I grabbed it to scan its pages for poems by John.

The other thing I envied was that William's school had a tuck shop, where William sometimes bought me stale marshmallow fish, a great delicacy—pale green or yellow or pink. If I slipped him enough of my pocket money, he would also bring home a tube of sherbet that you sucked through a thin liquorice straw. It didn't matter that it caught in your throat and made you cough.

There was something else that William's school brought me that my own could not—my first boyfriend.

He was a boarder in the KES boarding school at the top of the *kopje* behind our house and we met at a party when I was 13 and he gave me my first kiss. He had a rather large nose, which I thought only added to his attractiveness.

After that, he would often come down the hill, which was not allowed, and knock at the kitchen door.

"Let's have a swim, Cathy," he would say, giving me a hug and a kiss.

After the swim he was very happy to eat whatever cake or biscuits Ellen had baked for our tea. Sometimes he brought something other than an appetite for Ellen's baking.

"Look what I've brought you, Cathy, a flag I stole from the soccer team we played against this afternoon," and he pulled from his sweat pants a crumpled piece of material with the flag of a rival school.

Best of all, he sent me a letter during my exams. (KES had different holidays than Roedean's, so often when I was at school he was on holiday and vice versa, except for the summer holidays, which overlapped.) Inside he wrote how much he missed me and that he had found the enclosed four-leaf clover and was sending it to bring me luck. I immediately added it to my collection of mascots which sat on my desk for every exam I wrote from Lower V to Matric.

I was desolate when he broke up with me.

**

King Edward High School was a handsome collection of red brick creeper-covered buildings, with a great hall for assemblies and theatrical performances. It also had on its walls panel after panel of Honour Rolls.

WILLIAM AS JUNIOR MAYOR OF JOHANNESBURG.

One name stood out among all the others. It was the longest surname I had ever come across—John Katzenellenbogen-Adams.

I could not begin to live up to William's stellar career at school. Not only did he star in many of the school plays and lead the debating team to one victory after another in the inter-school tournaments, he was also very clever. He got five distinctions in Matric, one in every subject he wrote, except for Afrikaans.

I had managed a measly one, in French. I got a B for English, and scraped through on maths and Afrikaans, getting merely respectable marks for history and Latin.

Oh, and he was also Junior Mayor of Johannesburg in his last year at KES.

32—ROEDEAN

My high school, Roedean, a private school for girls, had delusions of grandeur. Its proudest boast was that it was established by the sister of one of the founders of Roedean in Brighton, England. Every morning at assembly, we prayed for "our sister schools in England and in Canada." We never discovered where exactly the Canadian "sister school" was, but we prayed for its wellbeing, nonetheless. I sometimes wondered if the Roedeans in Brighton and Canada prayed for their "sister school" in South Africa. I thought it rather unlikely.

THE LIBRARY WITH ITS BAY WINDOW. THE POST OFFICE TOWER IN THE BACKGROUND.

One of the delusions of grandeur involved the school requiring that any girl who aspired to enter its halls of wisdom first pass an entrance exam and interview with the headmistress, the dreaded and formidable Mrs. Joan Raikes. She was rumoured to be a fire-breathing dragon, who demolished entrance-examination girls for tea and spat the bones out of her study window.

Since my parents were very keen for me to attend this school, I had to go through the entrance exam ordeal—written exams in the morning and an interview with Mrs. Raikes in the afternoon.

On the day of the exam, I woke very early. I could not eat any breakfast and kept far away from the sight of William and his runny fried eggs. I put on my APPS uniform and Mom brushed and brushed my hair and then put it into two ponytails, neatly tied with blue ribbons. Then Grampa dropped me off at the school.

OFFICIAL MATRIC PHOTO, 1970. CATHY IS IN THE FRONT ROW, SECOND FROM LEFT, WITH THE LONG DARK PONYTAILS.

I looked around. There were several other girls in their school uniforms, looking just as lost as I was. There didn't seem to be anyone there to greet the girls doing their entrance exam.

"Where are we supposed to go?" we asked each other.

At last, a big girl in a navy tunic over a white blouse came up to us. "You must be the girls for the exam. Come this way."

We followed her to a large hall. A stern-faced woman with a long list in her hand asked us our names, checked us off her list and showed us to our places.

"There will be no talking until all the papers have been handed in. I will be watching you. If I catch anyone talking, they will have to leave this hall and this school, and they won't get a second chance."

I needed to go to the lav already, but didn't dare to ask because my Standard Five teacher had said that at Roedean you did not draw attention to the functioning of your bowels, even if you were bursting. How was I going to survive three hours of exam writing?

"You may turn your papers over," said the invigilator.

I looked at the questions and everything I knew ran out of my brain and down the stairs and out of the door as fast as it could. The lucky mascots I had brought with me and lined up on my desk didn't seem to be doing what they were supposed to. I was bursting, and in a cold sweat by the time the invigilator said, "Time's up. Hand in your papers. No talking till they are *all* in." My paper was filled with crossings out and handwriting that looked as if a herd of spiders had run amok.

As soon as we were outside the exam hall, the big girl came back and showed us where the school lavatories were. We stampeded. Then she conducted us to a place where we could eat our packed lunches. We sat nibbling our sandwiches and fruit and chocolate biscuits and talked about the exams.

"Wasn't that awful?"

"Oh no, don't tell me the answer to that maths question was 6? I put 7. Now I know I've failed."

Much too soon, I found myself in the headmistress's gloomy antechamber, waiting to be interviewed. Around me sat several other very nervous 12 year-olds. To my horror and mortification, I got the hiccoughs, not just genteel little ones, but huge, wracking ones that I could not control or suppress. I tried every trick I knew. I held my breath. I held my nose. I counted backwards from 300. Nothing worked. And the line of girls ahead of me kept getting shorter and shorter. Each one entered Mrs. Raikes's office looking like a scared rabbit and came out again a few minutes later looking stunned.

"I'll just die if I have hiccoughs when I'm in there with Mrs. Raikes," I said to the secretary. She didn't bother to respond.

Then she called my name, and I was ushered into The Presence. My hiccoughs stopped abruptly and completely. Mrs. Joan Raikes peered down over the tops of her half-moon glasses and spoke in her commanding and rather creaky English voice.

"Catherine, what do you want to be when you grow up?"

"A ballerina, Mrs. Raikes."

"Pah, all you South Africans are crazy about Ballet!" (with a triple emphasis on the B) "With your brains you should concentrate on the academic side of things."

And since this view was shared by my parents, I put aside my ballet shoes and my ballerina dreams. Instead, I concentrated on English, Latin, French and history.

Somehow, to my parents' delight and my surprise, I was accepted at the school and began there the following January in Lower Five 1 (The names of the classes were another thing the school imported from England. If I'd gone to a purely South African government school, I'd have been in Standard 6 or Form 1). Lots of my friends from APPS also got in to Roedean.

Like almost all schools, Roedean had a uniform. Ours was a navy tunic (not pleated, thank goodness!) and a white blouse with green and blue embroidery round the collar and sleeve edges. The summer blouses had short sleeves and the winter blouses had long sleeves. In winter, the tunic was of heavy cotton—in summer, it was a lighter fabric. The tunics could not be shorter than two inches above the knee, or else! In summer we wore a white panama hat with a green, white and navy ribbon on it—in winter, a navy hat with the same hatband, or a navy beret with the school badge. To finish the uniform off, we had to wear short brown socks in the summer, and long brown tights in the winter, and brown shoes—lace-ups, of course. I knew that *someone* had specially designed the uniform so we would all look as ugly as possible and no boy in the whole world would be tempted to flirt with us. It was not much comfort to think of the hideous uniform the girls at Helpmekaar, the Afrikaans High School, had to wear, with its brown-and-yellow striped blazers and matching ties.

For gym we wore navy wrap-around skirts, short-sleeved white cotton blouses, and black baggy bloomers over our regular underpants.

There was only one family of girls at the school who could wear their berets with any hint of panache—the McArthur sisters, Nicola, Lise, Pippa, and Monica, whose mother was French from Switzerland. I was sure that this was what gave them an instinctive flair in the wearing of clothes and particularly in the wearing of hats and berets. The rest of us felt ugly and embarrassed to be seen in such a get-up, and would remove the berets as soon we felt we were safe from the eagle eyes of the prefects supervising arrivals and departures from the school.

But there was one girl, Barbara, who actually looked beautiful in the school uniform. Rather, she was so beautiful that even the hideous school uniform could not make her look ugly. The rest of us hated and resented our uniforms and envied anyone who went to Hyde Park, which was co-ed *and* where you didn't have a uniform and could wear anything you liked to school.

Apart from the strange names of the classes, Roedean copied other English boarding school customs and traditions. The house system, prefects, and ghastly English institutional food, guaranteed to give us indigestion, lumpy figures, and blotchy complexions.

No fresh South African fruit and vegetables will be eaten here, thank you very much.

If your mother signed you up for hot lunch, you had to endure sitting at a table headed by a sadistic prefect who forced you to eat the disgusting substances put in front of you on pain of a housemark if anything was left on your plate. Certain days had certain foods. Monday was fried liver and onions, followed by boiled pudding drowning in lumpy custard, lukewarm, with the skin beginning to form on it. Tuesday was stringy beef accompanied by undercooked potatoes and over-boiled cabbage, and treacle pudding, with custard—probably the same custard as Monday's, reheated. From week to week we rotated tables, and once every two months or so, you found yourself seated at Mrs. Raikes's table. There you had to eat whatever was put in front of you, or Mrs. Raikes would fix you with her over-the-spectacles glare until you had eaten every mouthful.

Between the main course and dessert, the headmistress would read the names of the girls who had received letters that day, always a tense few minutes for the boarders. There were tears if your name was not read out, and laughter and smiles if you were one of the lucky ones whose family and friends had written to you. Mrs. Raikes would read out the names on the letters one at a time, in alphabetical order. Some girls seemed to get several every day, others only the occasional letter. And on Valentine's Day the suspense and the delight or the misery were even more intense A rumour went round one year that one not particularly pretty girl had asked her mother to send her 10 Valentine cards, all unsigned of course, in separate envelopes.

But if you were a daygirl with a sensible mother and a kind servant to prepare your school food, you didn't care about custard or letters from friends. Instead, you sat eating your lunch on Pleasaunce, unless the weather was too cold or rainy. Pleasaunce was a large grassy field bounded by a low stone wall with an unlocked gate in the middle. Sometimes the travelling African evangelist in his long white robe would come through the gate as we daygirls sat at lunch on the grass. He joked and sang and preached to us. Afterwards, he was happy to accept a sandwich or a piece of fruit or a slice of cake and be on his way.

**

CATHY IN THE MIDDLE, IN TENNIS CLOTHES, THE NAVY WRAPAROUND SKIRT CONCEALING
THE STATUTORY BLACK BLOOMERS WORN FOR ALL GAMES OTHER THAN SWIMMING.

I was put into St. Ursula's or Bears—the green house. Everyone who belonged to the house had to attend the house meeting once a month. The teacher in charge and the house prefect gave us stern lectures and exhortations about beating the other houses at games—tennis, swimming, netball, hockey, cricket—and not getting *Housemarks*, which would count against winning the cup at the end of the year. Negative Housemarks were awarded by teachers who found your work below standard or whom you cheeked. Prefects also relished the privilege of giving out Housemarks for anything or nothing, especially if they were having an off-day, which seemed to be a good deal of the time. But positive Housemarks could be won by excellence in sports.

Housenights were the house events of the year. The school had three terms, and each term, one of the houses would hold a Housenight. The head of the house, in consultation with other senior dignitaries, would decide on a theme, and the rest of the members of the house would have to provide the labour for decorations, and the talent for skits. Housenight included a costume parade by members of other houses, for which the winners received prizes. A feast, with lots of orange squash and strange food on the menu, was organized by the host House. You had to think of weird names to give the different dishes. Members of the host house entertained the rest of the school with skits.

One term, when it was Bears' turn to host Housenight, one of the girls did a striptease. A large sheet was hung up across the stage and a light shone on it. Behind the screen, the girl started off looking very bulky. She took off one item of clothing after another. When she was down to her bra and pants, everyone held their breath. Slowly she removed first her bra and then her underpants. She was totally naked! There were gasps from the audience. The teachers looked shocked. Only we knew that she had worn two bras and two pairs of underpants, and was actually still wearing a close fitting bikini. After some stifled giggles and huge applause, she stepped out from behind the screen and everyone could see she was still in her bikini. Of course, we never told our parents about that particular skit.

Something else we had to do at Housenight, apart from parades and skits and decorations and strange food, was to sing school songs. These were all taken from our "sister schools" and there were at least eight jolly tunes we had to sing. There was also a lugubrious one called *Forty Years On*. The one we all liked best was a hymn to the glory of our cricket team, which went something like "Oh, the cricket first eleven, we admire on every hand, 'Tis the one above all others, 'Tis the best in all the land. May their scores be never failing and their bowling ever true, oh noble first eleven, here's the best of health to you!"

All of us who didn't play cricket but had been forced to attend the matches, where we were almost always ignominiously defeated, just had to shriek with laughter.

There were other major Housenight traditions. After we had sung a few of the songs, there would be a pause. Then the Housemistress of Bears, or Lambs or Cats, whichever was hosting the Housenight, would say, very slowly and deliberately, "And now we will sing..." We said in unison, "the Song of the Howz-zes."

And when all the songs had been sung, and all the skits performed, and all the prizes handed out and supper finished, the same housemistress would say, very slowly and deliberately, "And now we will all go..." "Quickly and quietly to BED!" we shouted.

The boarders ran upstairs to their dormitories, and the daygirls rushed out to where their parents were waiting to fetch them outside the school gates.

**

Throughout my years at high school, I had frequent and torrential nosebleeds, which were particularly awful when they happened during exams. To makes things worse, the girl who sat in front of me in the examination hall—and it was always the same girl, because we were seated in alphabetical order—suffered from strangulated barking sneezes. In the middle of trying to answer an impossible history question or remember the particular theorem that would help you solve the rider in question 3, she would make a series of explosive sounds. I would swear with fright and annoyance, and my wits would fly out of the window.

Far more nerve-wracking than exams was the School Dance. We had one in Ante-Matric and one in Matric. If you did not have an older brother whose friends you could phone, you had (somehow) to find a boy on your own to take to the dance with you. There was nothing for it but to begin the *excruciatingly embarrassing* job of phoning up the brothers of your friends, one after another, until you found one who was prepared to come with you, sight unseen (on *both* sides!).

CATHY, IN THE TURQUOISE EGG DRESS, AND JOHN AT THE MATRIC DANCE.

"Hello, Peter, you don't know me, but my name is Cathy Kentridge and I'm in the same class as Erica. Would you be able to come to the school dance with me on the 8th of June?"

There was an embarrassed silence, me holding thumbs that he'd say yes, the boy, no doubt, running through all the reasons why he couldn't and wouldn't be able to escort me.

"Um, sorry…um, it's really nice of you to ask, but I have something else going on that evening. Bye."

"Hello, Andrew, you don't know me, but my name is Cathy Kentridge and I'm in the same class as Jennifer. I wonder if you would like to come to the school dance with me on the 8th of June?"

"Oh, um… didn't she tell you I already have a girlfriend? Bye."

Even worse than these phone calls, and the litany of refusals and excuses, was the prospect of my mother taking pity on me and trying to find me an escort from among the sons of her friends.

One year, I had to resort to this. Every single friend's brother I'd phoned was unable or unwilling to go to the dance with me. So my mother phoned her friend who phoned her friend who phoned her friend, whose son was prepared to come to the dance with me. When he came to the door to fetch me for the dance, he turned out to be short, fat, and lumpy, and he wore white shoes! I felt so embarrassed that I would be seen with him, let alone have to dance with him and spend a whole evening with him as my escort. The only thing that would have been worse than going to the dance with him was the humiliating prospect of being obliged to admit that you could not find a boy to invite to the dance and therefore would not be attending.

The one nice thing about the dances was the beautiful dress you wore. For my first school dance, my mother made me a dress with a shimmering white bodice and long sleeves, and an orange linen full-length skirt with a matching cummerbund. I wore this with a large shiny gold medallion on a chain that my father had brought me from the Metropolitan Museum in New York. My hair was in an updo, sprayed rigid by the hairdresser earlier that day.

As each couple arrived, the girl had to introduce her escort to the headmistress and then pose for an official photograph. (A few weeks later, when I got my photo, I cut it in half, so it only showed me, and a bit of his hand.) The teachers took turns to patrol the grounds with their torches at the ready, searching the bushes for couples who might be "getting off."

For the Matric dance, my mother made me a beautiful, v-necked, sleeveless, full-length dress of curtaining fabric, a white background with turquoise egg shapes on it. I went to this dance with John, who always made me laugh, rather nervously, when I saw him, and who had a small dog called Tinkles, who sat on a chair at the table and ate with the family. John was the brother of my friend Sally, so at least we had seen each other a few times before I screwed up my courage to invite him to the dance.

"Hello, John, this is Cathy Kentridge, Sally's friend. Yes, that was really funny when you were calling those madams pretending to be a servant answering the want ads. Um…I was wondering, could you come to the school dance with me on June 14th?"

"Yes, thank you. Would you like to meet before that, say next Saturday, and we could go to a film?"

This response was beyond my wildest dreams. We had a few dates in the weeks before the dance and started going out together, so I had the one-upmanship of bringing not a stranger but my boyfriend to the dance.

When the photos of that dance came back, I loved the ones of me and John dancing, and put them into a special album.

In the end, Roedean did something completely surprising and wonderful: it produced a boyfriend for me.

33—EXAMS

Exams were the worst. Worse than hockey or swimming with the sadistic games teacher, worse than science tests, almost worse than trying to find a boy to invite to the Matric Dance.

On exam mornings I woke up in a state of panic, having hardly slept the night before. Dates and formulas and theorems were rushing round and round in my head.

Grampa was in the kitchen when I came downstairs.

"*Boker Tov*, Lovey. *Tempus fugit*. You need to eat those scrambled eggs today. You need fuel so you can do well in the exam."

"But Grampa, I can't. It's choking me. O sies, William has runny yolk all over his chin, I feel sick."

By the time Ellen had put my lunchbox in my sack and it was time to get into Grampa's car, my stomach was in knots. We got to school far too soon.

Grampa waved goodbye, "Lovey, you will be fine. Just remember all the work we've done. Don't let your nerves win. I will be thinking of you at 8:30 and all through the exam."

I walked as slowly as I could to the Bears' cloakroom and hung up my raincoat. I dawdled over to the classroom. All the other girls seemed to be feeling pretty awful as well.

"I didn't sleep at all. Did you?"

"No, I threw up over breakfast," said Nicola.

"I couldn't finish my Coco Pops," said Shelley.

"I stayed up all night revising theorems. I know all of them. I'm not worried at all," said Vicky. She didn't have to worry. She always knew all of the theorems and equations.

After assembly, which was over much more quickly than usual, Madam told us it was time to take our seats as the exam would start in five minutes. "Put everything away except pens, pencils, and rubbers. And NO TALKING from now till I tell you to put down your pens."

She walked slowly along the rows of desks, handing out an exam paper to each girl. The paper was face down. You had to wait till she said, "You may turn the paper over and begin."

Carefully, I took my mascots out of their box and arranged them at the edge of my desk so that I could see them but they wouldn't get in the way of my exam papers. There were four mascots: a tiny troll with suede clothes and black wispy hair, a small Canada goose carved out of soapstone, a black cat charm, and a bell from Switzerland that you could put on a chain and wear around your neck. I had acquired all these mascots when I first went to high school at Roedean. They needed to be there for every exam. I had them from Lower V to Matric. I kept them in a special box with a gold lid. On each corner I wrote the name of the class I was in: Lower V, Middle V, Upper V, Antes, and in the middle, the final one, Matric. By then the box was held together by a rubber band. They were meant to bring me luck and make me not panic. But even they couldn't save me from the terrors of maths or history exams.

Something else that had to be on the desk during exams was a clock, so I could see how much time I had left to finish the paper. I'd carefully place it on the corner of my desk, beside the mascots. When it wasn't exam time, the clock lived on my bedside table, but not at night. The ticking would have kept me awake, so the clock went into a drawer or into the cupboard, muffled between layers of jerseys. But exams were different.

The alarm clock had to be wound up and the correct time set, with the hands moving slowly round the dial. For each exam, I would wind it and set it, and as the exam began I could hear it ticking. I glanced at it every few minutes to see how much time I had left. Almost always, I would be surprised at how slowly time was moving. "I still have 30 minutes left! I can't believe it!" and I'd put my head down and frown over the question that the history teacher or the French teacher or the Latin teacher had set. Suddenly the invigilator called, "Time up. Put down your pens and papers!" and I wouldn't be even half done! And I'd look up at the clock above the blackboard and realize that, once again, my clock had stopped half way through the exam.

Grampa had said he'd be thinking of me, especially during the maths exam, so I would remember the theorems and the equations and not get them all confused in my mind. I could *feel* him thinking about me and willing me to do well. I knew I could do the most complex equations and get the most obscure theorems to come out right when I was dong regular homework. And Grampa often helped me to understand the theorems and to puzzle out the algebra. But put me in front of an exam paper for a timed exam, and I would get them all muddled, and land up with very low marks, sometimes not even scraping through. While the numbers and theorems did crazy dances in my brain, I would be thinking in desperation how disappointed Grampa would be that I hadn't been able to shine at maths. Why oh why weren't his clear mathematical thoughts transmitting to my brain?

It didn't help that the sneezer was sitting in front of me, with her vast array of allergies and her shocking, loud sneezes that half frightened everyone out of their wits when they erupted during an exam, bursting the surrounding silence of panic, beating hearts, and brains working overtime.

History exams were almost as bad as maths. Maybe they were worse. There were two different Cathys. In class I was one of the brightest girls, always with something intelligent to say, and basking in the approval of our teacher. Yet during exams, my face would go white, and the Napoleonic wars would bump into each other, and victories and defeats would all be in the wrong places at the wrong times for the wrong reasons. And don't even mention the Boer Wars or Rorke's Drift or the Siege of Mafeking, and which trek was Piet Retief on and which Boer was betrayed to his death by Dingaan or was it Chaka Zulu?

I shone in only two types of exam. You couldn't get me to panic about French or English exams if you tried. I was fine. I blitzed through grammar and literature and essay papers, especially in French, attaining excellent marks, in spite of what I was convinced were the machinations of my French and English teachers to give me low marks on purpose.

The post mortems were almost worse than the exams themselves, especially when it had been a maths or history exam.

"That was *such* an easy paper," said Alice. "Did you get 33 for the answer to the first equation?"

I knew that I had not, and that her answer was right. She went on: "That rider was so simple. I finished the exam 20 minutes before Madam told us to put our pens down. I had time to check over every answer."

I hadn't even reached the last two questions on the paper.

It was the same story after history.

"I'm so glad we got that essay question on the Great Trek. I wrote down the names of all the important Boers who went on it, and the battles," said Mary.

I kept silent. I knew that I had got the names of the Great Trek Boers confused with the 1820 Settlers, or was it the Huguenots?

Just before the end of term came the dreaded reading of the marks, out loud, by the teacher of each subject, starting with the name of the person with the lowest marks. You sat there in a cold sweat, waiting for your name and your mark. If it came too early in the list, you knew you were at the bottom of the class – maybe you'd even failed. Of course, if it were maths, I *had* failed once or twice—and then your heart went into your mouth as the list went on. Maybe this time I'd be top in English (never), or French (once or twice), the French teacher reading out "Cath'rine Kentridge, 85%" with a grimace and audible sneer and disappointment in her voice. She would much rather one of the other girls had got that mark. 85% from her was like 105% from anyone else, since she was *so* pernickety about the marks. Every single accent, tense, masculine or feminine noun, adjective, and verb ending had to be correct or you got nothing!

Unlike at my brothers' school, we were not given positions in class, so there was never the race to be *first*. But we all knew who was first, and in which subjects.

There was no end to the horror of exams. It didn't end with writing the paper. It didn't end with the teachers reading the marks out loud. There was still one more awfulness to come: The School Report. The arrival of the report spoiled the start of every winter and summer holiday.

It was August, cold and dry, the start of the winter holidays, about 2 o'clock in the afternoon. I was at the bottom of the drive lying in wait for the postman to deliver my report in a large envelope with my parents' names on it, and with the return address of the school on the back. The maths exam had been particularly dreadful and I already knew how bad my marks were. As soon as the postman handed me the post, I ran up the drive and into my bedroom and closed the door. Then I opened the report and the full misery was there, in black and white, "maths: 39%." And even in the classes and exams where I knew I shone, French and English, neither teacher ever said anything positive or encouraging about me. But at least I could be prepared with excuses to give my parents about why the marks and comments were bad or poor.

Sometimes I wanted to destroy the Report unread, I was so afraid of what might be in it. But I didn't dare, because I knew my parents and the school would start asking questions if it went missing and I would be found out.

That evening, after supper, I handed the Report to Mom and Dad and watched their faces turn grim as they read it through, twice, before saying, "What happened? You can do better than this."

JACARANDA TREES AT THE BOTTOM OF THE DRIVE.

34—FRIENDS

My brothers, William and Matthew, like our father and uncles before them, went to King Edward VII Preparatory School and King Edward VII High. Since the schools were just up the hill, not only could they walk to and from school when they were old enough, but all their friends lived within biking or walking distance.

My high school, Roedean, was much closer to where I lived than APPS had been. You *could* walk there, but it would be a long walk along a very busy street, or you could take the bus. Walking or taking the bus were not something to be done daily—but only rarely and out of great necessity.

All my friends, except Sari-next-door, lived far away, because the girls who attended Roedean came from all over Johannesburg's far-flung suburbs and all the provinces of South Africa.

At Auckland Park, there was Sally, the very clever daughter of Len, an English professor, who was also from England, and his wife Pat, who I thought looked down her nose at me as if I were a bad smell. Whenever I was in their car or at their house, I would hear myself saying all kinds of things that just popped out of my mouth and that I had far better not have said, such as swear words, which were standard language amongst ourselves at school, but were never to be uttered in the presence or within earshot of parents.

Sally was very sophisticated. She could understand the humour in "Beyond the Fringe," and explain it to me, and she could understand the songs of the French singer, Françoise Hardy, whose songs we listened to day and night. Best of all, she knew which Beatle was singing in any particular Beatles' song.

Almost worth the disapproval I would endure at Sally's house was the prospect of seeing her older brother, John. I had a bit of a crush on John. I always hoped he would be there and notice me. I found his sense of humour very funny and daring.

He would phone up "madams" who had placed "help wanted" ads in the paper. He pretended to be a servant looking for work.

"Hello, Madam, it's Elsie. I was looking in your ad. I want to work for you, eh heh, yes, madam. I am a very good gerl. I work very very hard," said John.

Sally and I listened in the background, trying not to giggle. To us his words and accent sounded totally convincing.

At other times, he would phone a random number and when the person answered he would say, "Is your fridge running?"

"Yes," said the voice at the other end.

"Quick, you better run after it before it runs out of the door."

John hung up quickly.

Sally and I collapsed with hysterical laughter.

At Roedean, I had a love-hate friendship with one of the girls. Our parents were close friends and, occasionally, her mother would give me a lift home in her Jaguar. She always asked us about our marks in the latest school test.

"I got eight out of 10 for Latin," I would say, feeling a little embarrassed.

"Well done, Cathy. What did you get, Tessa?"

"Seven."

"Why can't you be as clever as Cathy?"

These remarks were not guaranteed to make Tessa like me. So sometimes we were friends and sometimes we were not. When it was 'on', we had sleepovers at each other's houses, talked till midnight and raided our mothers' store cupboards, which were filled with nuts, dried fruit, chocolate, and Provita crackers.

Tessa's house was luxurious, with at least four bathrooms and a fancy guest suite. My whole family was often invited for an evening of old black and white films shown on 8mm projectors on a huge screen. There we saw The Marx Brothers' films and Lawrence Olivier in *Hamlet* and *King Henry V* and enjoyed their Ellen's chocolate cake.

Heidi, whom I had met at an art camp on a farm several hours' drive from Johannesburg, came to Roedean in my second year there. One afternoon at camp, Heidi locked herself into the girls' bathroom, with me as her frightened but excited accomplice. She took a pair of scissors to her long hair and hacked it off, till it was an uneven length, just below her ears.

"My mother will give me hell when she sees this. But I don't care. Let her!"

H's mother was Afrikaans, her father absent and Portuguese from Mozambique.

Heidi and her mother and brother lived in a small flat in Hillbrow, a seedy, down-at-heel part of Johannesburg. Her mother was always pleasant and generous to me and bought me beautifully-illustrated art and ballet books from Exclusive Books in Hillbrow. The thing I cherished most about H's mother was her use of English.

"I'll just clobber this ice-cream into four pieces," she would say, handing me a huge bowl of vanilla with chocolate sauce.

Heidi was a champion swimmer, with a swimmer's broad shoulders. She had been working on her Hope Chest since she could thread a needle. As the years passed, it grew fuller and fuller of embroidered tablecloths and napkins, and then of homemade clothes, beautifully made, but unfashionable. She also sewed for her friends—she made me an exquisite needlepoint change purse, decorated with my initials and a butterfly.

Nicola was another friend from Roedean. When I first met her, she lived in a small house in Houghton, not too far from mine. She had three sisters and a brother, John, on whom they all doted. Her mother, Ouida, was Swiss, and always plaited her hair into two long braids and wound them round the top of her head.

For some reason, I was very afraid of Nicola's father. Far too often, when I invited Nicola to do something with me like come to my house for lunch or to swim she would say, "I'd love to, but Daddy won't let me." Whenever I visited Nicola, I lived in dread that he would appear. Sometimes, just when I thought I was safe, I'd hear his voice, and his tall, thin red-haired and moustachio-ed figure would appear round the door. I cowered in a corner, trying to make myself invisible, terrified that he would say something to me. I longed for my mother to fetch me so that the visit could end.

Nicola and her sisters were forbidden to cut their hair, though they were allowed to have the split ends trimmed occasionally. We could not understand why it was a matter of life or death to him that they did not cut their hair.

One afternoon, when we were about 16, Nicola and I went to the hairdresser. Trembling, but determined, Nicola asked the hairdresser to cut her hair short. It was an amazing transformation, and made Nicola look even prettier.

But when she got home, her mother went into hysterics, and when her father returned from his chambers (he was an advocate), he poured out his wrath upon her, told her "Your so-called friend, Cathy, is no longer welcome in this house," grounded Nicola for three months—and carried out the grounding to the last day.

Later Nicola and her family moved to a wonderful house, at the top of Houghton Drive, across from The Wilds. There they had more than enough space for everybody including the two elderly Swiss ladies, a grandmother and a great-aunt, to whom the house belonged. The house had a huge and wild garden, and orchards with apricot and peach trees. The girls and the women made delicious peach jam and apricot jam, with the pips in it to give it a tang of bitterness amid the sweetness.

My best friend was Jane, the dancer. Jane's mother was a teacher at the Teachers' Training College in Johannesburg, and she was totally on the side of her daughters' dancing careers. No school with long hours and a daunting headmistress was going to ruin their chances. Mrs. Pick helped Jane and her sister Diana with their homework, and fought and won their battle to be allowed to miss school from time to time so they could have ballet lessons and Spanish dancing lessons and take part in dance exams and competitions.

And when it came to the social life of her daughters, Jane's mother had a much more free and easy approach to parenting than mine.

There was none of the, "You have to be home by 11 or else…"

Once, when I was about 15, I went to visit Jane. With her mother's consent, we took the train on our own to Germiston. This was a one-horse industrial town about half an hour's ride outside Johannesburg, and the home of Jane's boyfriend, Corrie. I had told my mother I was going to play tennis, with not a word about Germiston.

It was just my bad luck that my mother phoned to say she would be fetching me at four instead of five. Jane's mother said, "Oh, the girls won't be back by then. They've gone to Germiston on the train."

My mother was furious, and so was my father when she told him. Visits to each other's houses were forbidden for several months.

Jane had two Chihuahuas who slept at the foot of her bed, inside the covers. Jane's father, who was much older than her mother, was a crusty Scotsman who ran a dry-cleaning business. I was very surprised to hear that he had once been a well-known Scottish dancer. A father who danced in a kilt?

Jane always had scores of boyfriends clamouring to go out with her. She had that marvellous and magical quality, sex-appeal, which led to the brief period when we were 'unfriends'. I gave a party and there was one boy there whom I fancied and was determined to be kissed by before the evening was over. But instead of kissing me, he spent the evening with Jane somewhere outside in the dark garden.

And then there was Sari, the girl next door. Sari was an Afrikaner. To get to Sari's, I climbed a narrow path at the back of Number 72, went through a gap in the hedge, and followed the path down to the kitchen door of her house. Sari lived with her mother, and her stepfather, a wealthy right wing businessman with a bristly little moustache.

A few years after Sari moved in next door, he demolished the old house and built a new one that looked like a giant white matchbox perched on the hill. He erected a slave bell, like the ones they used to use in America and in the Cape to summon slaves to work. He also put up a sculpture of a seated woman at the bend in the drive. The sculpture was white concrete, but looked as if it was made out of a melting block of Walls' Vanilla ice-cream, which, we all believed, had more whale oil and soap by-products in it than real milk or cream.

Sari and I were about the same age and we both loved the Beatles. Sari invited me to my first ever 'mixed' party. Mixed meant boys and girls, as Sari went to a co-ed school. But they all spoke Afrikaans at the party and I was paralyzed with shyness and my inability to speak Afrikaans with any kind of fluency. I dreaded being asked to dance by any of the shy and pimply boys whom Sari had invited. I far preferred dancing on my own to a Beatles' record in Sari's living room when we were practising for the party.

Sari had a swimming pool at her house long before we put in ours. So on summer afternoons, I went over to her place for tanning and swimming. We lay frying in suntan lotion at the side of Sari's pool, gossiping about the boys at her school—there weren't any at mine—and, occasionally, getting up to cool off with a length or two of the pool, or to pick Catawba grapes from the vines that fringed it.

Sari's mother was very pretty, with blonde hair in a soft bun. But I was deathly afraid of her. She accused Fluffy, one of our family cats, of tormenting her cat and threatened to shoot him. I had no doubt she would carry out her threat if she wanted to. Sari had shown me where her mother kept her gun. Fluffy was furry, fat, fixed, and friendly. Nevertheless my family took the threat seriously, and kept Fluffy locked up till Sari's mother calmed down.

When Sari's mother was not in cat-killing mode, she was friendly and offered me her homemade Melktert, which was a traditional Afrikaner delicacy. Its main ingredient was boiled sour milk and the very thought of it, let alone the smell, made me turn green.

Not only did Sari provide Beatles' songs to dance to and boys to fear at parties, she also often did my hair up into a bun before ballet on Saturdays. Then she pinned a hair net over it, so that the beautiful bun nestled neatly at the nape of my head, and I felt like a real ballerina.

Sometimes I was friends with Wendy, an American with a profile like a hawk. She spoke, of course, with an American accent, which we all admired and envied. She introduced me to two things: moisturizer, Elizabeth Arden's Blue Grass, which just made my skin greasier than it was already, and American records. She knew all about the latest records from 'The States' and would invite me over to her house to listen to them. We spent hours listening to Buffy St. Marie, and Jefferson Airplane, and to songs like *Broken Arrow*. She occasionally allowed me to borrow records so I could play them at home.

The trouble was, going to her house meant running the risk of meeting her brother. He was a few years older than Wendy, and I was very afraid of him. If he so much as looked at me, never mind spoke to me, I burst into nervous hysterics and had to rush into Wendy's bedroom and slam the door shut.

**

There was something about being at Roedean and trying to make friends outside of school, especially with boys. Roedean girls had a reputation for snobbishness. The daygirls did at any rate. The boarders told us often and loudly that they were desperate to "get off" with boys. From what they said, they spent their holidays snogging their faces off with the local boys, and their school nights planning, and sometimes actually managing to have, assignations with boys from the nearby boys' boarding school.

At the rare mixed parties that I went to as a teenager, I pretended I went to some school other than Roedean. But my accent was a dead giveaway. A boy would come up to ask me to dance, introduce himself and then, sure enough, ask the question I dreaded.

"So, where do you go to school?"

If I admitted that I went to Roedean, two things invariably happened: first he backed away and second he began to mock my accent. Strangely, it was no stigma for a boy to admit that he went to one of the posh boys' private schools like St. Stithian's or St. John's – in fact there was a certain cachet for any girl about having a boyfriend, or at least, a dance partner, who attended one of those schools.

At my school, there were some girls who were friends only when there was a party involved. These were the popular girls, and if word got around that they were coming to your party, you knew it would be a success. They would keep you in suspense, waiting to see if a better invitation came up, and if it didn't, they would come to your party. As soon as the party was over, and everyone and everything had been thoroughly gossiped over, these girls reverted to ignoring me or saying things like, "You look like such a spaz on the tennis court doing all that ballet and running on tiptoes to hit the ball."

It was one thing to go to someone else's mixed party and try to find a boy to go with if it was a 'couple's' party. The killer was trying to have a mixed party of your own. By the time I was 15, there was no way I could have thrown an all-girls' party. The sneering and mockery would have been endless. So if I wanted to have a party *and* to have people come to that party, I had to somehow, somewhere, come up with some boys to invite.

I spent hours agonizing over this with my friends.

"Jane, what am I going to do? I've invited eight girls, but I've only got five boys so far. Do you know any whom you could ask?"

"There are some I still know from my old school. But I don't know if they'd come to a party with *Roedean* girls."

If the party night were drawing close and there still were not enough boys, I might have to ask my mother to ask her friends if any of their sons would come to my party. But that request was definitely a last resort.

On party night, things generally worked out all right, even if I was more often a wallflower, in my pale lipstick and Mary Quant mini dress, than a dancer. And sometimes I was lucky and a boy I liked would ask me for a slow dance, holding me tightly and kissing me while we swayed in the darkness to a sexy French song which Sally had had to explain to us. When that song played, I was glad that the lights were dim and that my hovering parents didn't speak French.

35—PLAY ACTING

At William's school, you saved your acting talents for the school plays and the debating society. At Roedean, you used your acting talents every day in all kinds of ways—at least *I* did.

Of course, I acted in real plays. I was Emily in a playreading of *Our Town*. Our director told us not to try and put on American accents, but just to use our own voices and put as much thought and emotion into the words as possible. But one of the girls insisted on putting on an American accent—at least *she* thought it sounded American. The rest of us winced and covered our ears and made sarcastic comments,

"If that's American, I'm speaking Greek!"

But no amount of teasing had any effect. She continued to do her 'American' voice. I was glad she had only a small part. I felt very proud to have such a large role as Emily, and one where I could use so many different emotions.

We also did a playreading of Dylan Thomas's *Under Milkwood*. Sally was the one who worked out the joke in the name of the town.

"Hey, did you know that Llareggub is bugger all spelt backwards?"

My star turn, at least what I thought was going to be my star turn, was as Puck in the school production of *A Midsummer Night's Dream*. We did the show in my last year at Roedean, when I was in Matric. At the dress rehearsal, in front of the assembled school, I made my grand entrance in green leotard, tights and ballet slippers, on a *grand jeté*. It launched me straight out of the wings onto my behind and off the stage at downstage right, to howls of laughter from the audience. Apparently the cleaning ladies had been very busy polishing the stage that morning.

The first night performance, therefore, was much less flamboyant, as I struggled to hide the pain in my coccyx. I also struggled not to catch the eye of my boyfriend, smiling and grimacing in the front row and doing his best to distract me, in a long scene where I had to remain 'hidden' in front of the stage left proscenium while the lovers went astray in the woods.

But I saved my greatest performances, moving myself to tears, to avoid having to write science or maths tests or to get off going to hockey practice.

I hung my head, and spoke in a small voice, as if I were trying to sound brave and not make a fuss,

"Madam, I feel so awful, my head is hurting... My stomach is hurting tooI feel queasy... ." I let my voice trail off, sounding as if I were about to burst into tears. Madam sent me to matron, who let me lie down in the San for an hour or so. By then I was feeling a lot better and the maths or science test or hockey practice was safely over.

Of course, I couldn't use this method to get out of games too often. I realized the teachers might begin to get a bit suspicious if I did. One of the types of games we all loathed was swimming. Miss Pumfrey made us do length after length of the cold school pool, in all kinds of weather, and didn't care if you said you had a cramp or were tired or ill. The only thing that could get you out of swimming was "The usual reason" i.e., being on your period.

Sally, Tessa, Nicola, and I put our heads together. We knew it was no use asking our mothers to write sick notes for us to give Miss Pumfrey. They simply wouldn't do it. Besides, they would have a pretty good idea of when we really had our periods. We decided that Sally should write the notes for us whenever necessary. She was the one who had the most grown-up writing and could use words that might really sound like the words ours mothers would use, and she could do a flourishing cursive signature.

At Monday's swimming lesson, I went up to Miss Pumfrey and handed her a note, without saying anything. It read:

"Please excuse Cathy Kentridge from swimming today, for the usual reason. Thank you." It was signed "F.N. Kentridge."

Miss Pumfrey gave me an ill-natured look and said, "All right, you may be excused. But you have to sit and watch anyway."

On Wednesday, Nicola went up to Miss Pumfrey and silently handed her a note, which read: "Dear Miss Pumfrey, please excuse Nicola from games for the usual reason, which always makes her feel very unwell. Thank you." It was signed "O. MacArthur."

CATHY AS PUCK, WITH GREEN POINTED EARS IN *A MIDSUMMER NIGHT'S DREAM*. DAIRIN IS OBERON, PIPPA AND MAZ ARE HER MINIONS. JULIA IS TITANIA. GILLIAN, ERICA, KAREN, VICKY, AND XANTHE ARE IN HER FAIRY TROUPE.

Then for a week or so, we would attend the swimming lessons and actually get into the pool and take our time doing lengths.

But we soon began again with our 'usual reasons', Sally making sure her handwriting and the signatures were a little different on each note.

**

The very best acting that happened while I was at Roedean didn't happen in any performance I did, on or off stage. It was the time we had a school trip across the road and up the hill to St. John's, the posh boys' school. We sat in the courtyard on a cold summer evening watching *Hamlet*. Or rather watching Philip de Ville as Hamlet. Phillip was tall and fair, and utterly dishy. Tears poured down my face as he lay dead on the cobblestones and Horatio said, "Good night sweet prince and flights of angels sing thee to thy rest." I had never seen such wonderful acting. He was better than Laurence Olivier in the black and white film I had seen so many times at Tessa's house. I wanted to rush out of my seat, and take him in my arms and tell him how much I adored him.

But I didn't dare, and went home to dream about him instead.

CATHY AT HER FIRST SCHOOL DANCE, IN
THE *EXCISED ESCORT* PHOTO, WEARING
THE WHITE AND ORANGE DRESS MADE BY
MOM AND THE GOLDEN PENDANT FROM
THE METROPOLITAN MUSEUM

36—TEACHERS

At Roedean, we had to address the teachers as 'madam', just as our servants at home had to call our mothers 'madam'. The teachers were madam whether they were married or single, and whether they were old or young. Many of the madams at Roedean came from England.

One of them was the English grammar teacher. She drilled the rules so deeply into our heads that we couldn't forget them, still less break them, even if we wanted to. We had hard-covered notebooks filled with the rules of English grammar; we had regular weekly grammar tests, and we had grammar exams twice a year.

"Girls, you must *never* write, 'Struggling to the top of the hill she fell off the cliff.' And anyone who writes, 'He wanted to quickly run away,' will get a housemark for splitting the infinitive!"

The grammar teacher was also head of the house called St. Agnes or Lambs. At one of the house meetings a new girl, a boarder, put up her hand to ask a question.

"Madam, why are there so few exeats? Why can't we go home every weekend?"

"Why do you think you are here? *If* your parents had wanted you to be at home, they would never have made you a boarder."

The girl burst in tears, and so did most of the girls around her. Perhaps their parents really didn't want them at home?

We had two Afrikaans teachers at Roedean. One of them, Juffrou, had hair that was dyed bright orange and she wore it in a beehive. She had a large nose, very thin legs, a large bum, a large bust, and a bulging stomach. She was always dressed in the height of vulgarity. She liked to take us into her confidence.

"Gurrls, I have to wear a two-way because I'm a bit broad in the beam."

We sniggered and nodded.

The "gurrls" learned nothing whatever in her classes except some shadowy details of her wedding night, which made us all feel very embarrassed.

The one thing she was good at was organizing parties in class. These took place during the last Afrikaans lesson of each term. Our job was to bring treats for the party. She merely gave commands and ate the food.

"Gurrls, don't tell anyone, but let's have a party on the last day of term. Cathy, you can bring chips, Sally you can bring Fanta. Pam can bring Coke and sweets. "

We soon found out that she said this to every class she taught, and that she landed up having more end-of-term parties than anyone.

She was a complete contrast to the other Afrikaans teacher, Mevrou. Mevrou had pale blonde hair which she wore in a bun, and a soft, pleasant voice. In Lower Five, the first year of high school, she made Afrikaans fun, though a lot of work. But in the last two years of school, Mevrou became panicked and tyrannical because she was afraid all her girls would fail. And you could not matriculate without passing Afrikaans. Suddenly, her pleasantness evaporated and she began to shout at us.

"Girls, if you don't do your homework and learn those *Anglicismes*, you will all fail Matric and you'll have to stay here for another year and it will be *all your fault!*"

"Anglicismes" were impure expressions imported into the *taal* from the English language and which the *taalpuriste* were trying so hard to eradicate. You had to master lists of proverbs and sayings such as "val met die duur in die huis" (to get straight to the point). And there were long lists of words for essays we were supposed to write on "Op die plaas" (on the farm`) or "My Vakansie" (my holiday) or "'n Middenag Fees" (a midnight feast). Mevrou would dictate the words to us; we would memorize them and then gabble the phrases to her as fast as we could when called upon to perform. We didn't even bother to make complete sentences.

"die strand, die see, my swem kostuum, my sandale, roomys, sonneskyn, braaivleis, piekniek " (the sand, the sea, my swimming costume, my sandals, ice cream, sunshine, barbecue, picnic.)

One of the few teachers who wasn't from England taught English and history in the early years of high school. We joked about her odd pronunciation:

"Please Madam, is it "RAY bid pap-ists" or rabid PAPE-ists"?

Mrs. John taught us history for the last two years of high school. Privately, we called her Gilly because her first name was Gillian. To her face, of course, she was 'Madam'. She had been a University lecturer before coming to Roedean, so her expectations of us were very high. She made history a riveting subject. And she liked to ask questions that would really get her students thinking about the subject. I did brilliantly in class at the oral response portion of the lessons. But come exam time, it was a different story. I went white with anxiety and panic, and the history dates rushed about in disorder behind my eyes, as the date of the First Great Trek got hopelessly confused with the British North America Act and Napoleon's deportation to St. Helena.

In history, as in all other subjects, except English and maths, it was as if there was one person in class, bright and confident, and a totally different person who panicked in exams. With maths, I was not much good in class and even worse in exams. I was always good at English.

We had a different English teacher for literature and composition. From almost the first lesson, Sally and I realized that she was not going to like us because we were 'too clever'. My English marks from her on my end of term reports were always far below what everyone knew they should be, and even from what they were on my homework. Somehow, she would turn the As and Bs she had given me in my exercise books into Cs and Ds on my reports.

At our third lesson with her, Sally, Erica, and I discovered the secret of her method of teaching English poetry.

Erica had a big sister, Ursula, who was two years ahead of us at school. I happened to have bought Ursula's poetry textbook. The book had scribbled notes in the margin for the teacher's special method of analyzing poetry. Her method, she proudly told us, was called SIFT, which stood for Sense, Intention, Form and Tone. Very soon, with Ursula's book in our hands, Erica, Sally, and I were able to prompt the teacher whenever she was stuck for the perfect word to describe or explain something in one of the set poems.

"What's the word I'm looking for to describe the Sense of Wordsworth's sonnet?"

"Madam, how about visionary?" one of us would say, glancing at Ursula's notes in the margin.

"That's it exactly."

Next day, we would be studying Coleridge's *Christobel*.

"Girls, what would you say the Intention of this poem is?"

"How about to hint at something terrifying?" Sally would say as I passed Ursula`s book to her.

"That's it exactly."

We smiled secretly and triumphantly at each other. It was clear that Madam had had the same thoughts and used exactly the same words from one year to the next to the next.

The senior French teacher at Roedean had come from Scotland decades before, but her accent sounded as if she had just stepped off the boat. We inherited her sneering Scottish accent for French. She terrified French into generations of girls at Roedean and kept them in a state of nervous hysteria, especially when they had forgotten a book they would need in class.

Every school holiday, she gave us homework to do, usually in the form of five or six poems to memorise. None of the other teachers would have dreamed of doing such a thing. On the first day back at school, we were expected to be ready to recite the French poems we had learned over the holidays.

"Bonjour, mes élevès. Avez-vous passez des bonnes vacances? Bon! Et maintenant, mes enfants, au travail!"

She looked over her spectacles at the class. She began to call out names, not going alphabetically or by row. Instead, she would pounce on girls at random, so that we were all in a tremble of anxious expectation. Just minutes before class we could recite the poems word- and accent-perfect for each other. But at Madam's pounce, we would be reduced to stammering idiots.

"Catherine Kentridge, I might have known you wouldn't have bothered to master your work. I think I am going to faint. Take a housemark and go straight to Mrs. Raikes."

In the Headmistress's office I stood there shaking. Mrs. Raikes looked over her spectacles at me: "Cathy, you should know better than not be prepared with your poems for her." And she sent me away without any punishment and with a hint of a smile on her face.

Our Latin teacher was totally different. She was a German Jewish refugee, with naturally orange hair, thick glasses, and orthopedic devices on the soles of her shoes. She taught me, and a dwindling number of others, for five years. 'Doc' Jacobs did her best to make Latin fun, while drilling the rules and their myriad exceptions into our unwilling brains.

On the last day of every term, she came smiling into the classroom clutching a magazine under her arm.

"Girls, I have a treat for you. It is a Latin newspaper for children. It is called *Acta Diurna* and comes all the way from England."

"Madam, please can we play hangman first?"

After a few rounds of hangman, in Latin, we struggled through some of the stories in *Acta Diurna*. Doc Jacobs' favourite parts were the cartoons. She laughed and laughed. But by the time she had explained and translated them, they were as dry as dust and we sat looking blankly at her wondering what was supposed to be so funny?

We studied Catullus and Ovid and the compulsory Caesar and his "All Gaul is divided into three parts" We also studied the legend of Psyche and Cupid from Apuleius's *Golden Ass*. Doc Jacobs pronounced Psyche as 'pesooshee'. Of course, the version used at Roedean was rigorously bowdlerized to make it suitable for young ladies. (The text for *Hamlet*, which we studied for two years, was cut down to about two acts, for the same reason.) Now and then Doc Jacobs would refer us to the complete and unabridged version, in English translation, "so you can find out what the real reward was that Venus gave for finding where Psyche was hiding." The reward that we found in the translation in the library was, "two exquisite thrusts of her tongue between their lips."

I discovered I had a talent for translating French and Latin into English. Madam did not appreciate my rendering of *à pas de loups* as 'pussyfooting'; Doc Jacobs thought my lively version of *The Legend of Psyche and Cupid* was very good.

Our science teacher was another of the school's British imports. She wore cat-shaped glassed with very thick lenses. She told us she had come out to South Africa solely so that her beloved and obese golden lab, Bonnie, would live longer—something her vet in England had promised.

Madam whistled her essess. Sally worked out a sentence with as many esses as possible for us to whisper to each other during class or at any other time as the mood took us.

"Ssssixty Ssseven sssentimetarssss ssssusspended on a ssssspring balansssse."

The lab was an evil-smelling room, bristling with burettes, pipettes,

Bunsen burners, and spring balances and their contents. I was completely out of my element in the science lab; I could not get any of my experiments to work; I couldn't even get the spring balance to balance, and had no idea how to do the science homework. I was not one of Madam's favourite pupils. She took exception to my poor experiments. She even took exception to my appearance, in the school-issue navy-blue zippered fleece jacket.

"Cathy, you look like SSSSSally from our alley."

I dropped science as soon as I was allowed to do so. But I did not manage to get rid of the whistling esses so easily. A year or so later, Madam and Bonnie, who accompanied her everywhere, turned up in the maths class. Apparently if you could teach science you could also teach maths. Bonnie spent the lessons sniffing our sacks, the brown sturdy canvas bags which contained all our books. Whenever his nose smelt out some chocolate, he paused and started to drool. Madam pounced on the girl to whom the sack belonged and forced her to give her chocolate to Bonnie, dealing out a negative housemark at the same time.

One morning there was a message pinned to the notice board outside the library. "Bonnie passed away peacefully in his sleep last night."

Soon afterwards the ssssscience teacher went back to England, to be replaced by the unheard of and exciting addition of a man to the school staff to teach science. All the girls he taught immediately developed a crush on him, and those who had dropped science began to wish that they had persevered.

**

When I returned to the school for Foundation Day just over a year after I had matriculated, I got a surprise. My English teacher and my French teacher were all smarmy congratulations. In that year I had matriculated with a distinction in French, obtained two A-levels in six months, with a distinction in French at a school in England and had been accepted to read English at Oxford.

"Catherine Kentridge," said one, with ill-concealed amazement, "I hear you have been sweeping all before you."

"*You* got accepted to read English at Oxford?" said the other. "I always knew you were the brightest girl in the school at English."

EPILOGUE

I left South Africa right after I wrote Matric, in December 1970, and went to school in England for a year to take A-levels and Oxford entrance. I had not wanted to go straight from high school at Roedean to starting a BA at the University of the Witwatersrand in Johannesburg. The plan was that I would have that year away from Johannesburg and then start at Wits in January 1972.

I was 17, William was 15, Eliza was 8, and Matthew was 6. The family went on a skiing holiday in Austria and then took me to England for my interview at Marlborough.

I was accepted and began A-Levels there in January 1971. Going to school in England turned out to be a turning point in my life. After A-Levels, I wrote the Oxford Entrance Exams. I was offered a place at Oxford, and returned to Johannesburg to fill in the 10 long months between my acceptance into Oxford, and my going up there, to Lady Margaret Hall, in October 1972.

So my childhood in South Africa ended when I wrote Matric, even though I attended Wits briefly to work on my essay-writing skills and to study French and Italian for a few months.

Since then I have lived in England and Canada, with brief returns to live in South Africa in my 20s. For years in England I tried to forget about or hide the fact that I was South African as it caused such trouble. People would jeer at you and make such negative assumptions if you told them you were South African. They also always told you what was wrong with South Africa and how it could be fixed. But they also made it clear they would not dream of going there to see what it was really like there because "it's against my conscience to support that regime."

I emigrated to Canada more than 30 years ago. Sometimes, my childhood in South Africa seems another lifetime away. At other times, it is as vivid and close as yesterday.

GLOSSARY

Afikomen: The piece of Matzo that is hidden during the Seder meal, at Passover, and must be ransomed by the leader of the Seder, since the meal cannot end until everyone has had a bite of the Afkikomen.

Ante-Matric: Penultimate year of high school

Bantu: A catch-all word for Africans, used in expressions such as 'Bantu Education' and 'Radio Bantu' and 'The Bantu People'.

Biltong: A South African delicacy of dried meat seasoned with salt and coriander seeds. You could get beef, ostrich, or game biltong. A favourite 'padkos' (food for the road) on any picnic or trip by car or train, and actually, at any time!

Biscuit: What North Americans call a cookie.

Blatjang: The Afrikaans word for chutney.

Boerewors: An Afrikaans word meaning literally 'farmer's sausage', made of beef and seasoned with coriander seeds. An essential food at a braaivleis.

Boker Tov: 'Good morning' in Hebrew.

Braai: Afrikaans for barbecue; used as a noun and as a verb.

Braaivleis: Literally 'barbecue meat'. Word used by all South Africans for a barbecue.

Bunking: Playing hooky, playing truant, usually from school.

Bymekaar: Afrikaans word for 'together' or 'side by side'.

Candy Floss: Cotton candy.

Charoset: A traditional food eaten at Passover. It is made of chopped-up apples, nuts, cinnamon, and sugar, moistened with wine.

Coloured: The word in general use in South Africa to designate people of mixed race, specifically 'Cape Coloureds'.

Cookies: What North Americans call cupcakes.

Dagga: Marijuana

Die Aamborstige Klok: Title of a book, Afrikaans, meaning "The Asthmatic Clock."

Die Skarlaken Eskade: Title of a book, Afrikaans, meaning "The Scarlet Squadron."

Doek: Afrikaans for headscarf, the head covering worn by all African women.

Eikona: Equivalent of North American "oh-oh," but a bit stronger.

Exeat: Official leave of absence from school for boarders at weekends or half-term.

Fiemies: Pickiness over food, origin unknown

Games: All-purpose word for school sports – tennis, hockey, netball, cricket, swimming.

Gefilte fish: A traditional Jewish dish of minced fish, usually stockfish.

"Hoe ry die boere sit sit so, sit sit so, sit sit so, hoe ry die boere sit sit so, sit sit so, hoerrah!" Words to an Afrikaans song, meaning "How the farmer rides, sitting just so, hurrah!"

Juffrou: Afrikaans for 'Miss'.

Kneidlach: Dumplings made of Matzo meal, served in chicken soup at Passover.

Kopje: Afrikaans word for hill.

Lav: Short for lavatory, used instead of toilet, which was regarded as rather affected.

Matric: Final year of high school. It also referred to the school-leaving exam you wrote in that year.

"Maar eers… Lav toe." Afrikaans, meaning "but first, [I must go] to the lavatory."

Mebos: Afrikaans word for fruit leather, generally made of dried peaches, apricots, or guavas, flattened and rolled up in many layers.

Melktert: Milk Tart, a traditional Afrikaans dessert of boiled milk, eggs, and seasoning.

Mevrou: Afrikaans for Mrs.

Mielie: Afrikaans for corn on the cob, used by Afrikaans and English-speaking South Africans

Mielie-Meal: Meal or flour made out of mielies, a staple food of Africans and often eaten with meat and gravy.

Naartjies: Afrikaans word, in general usage, for clementine.

Off: A servant's 'day off' was the one day in the week when he or she was not working. The day was sacrosanct, and could only be changed for emergencies. "Don't come over for tea. Ellen is off today so there won't be any fresh baking."

Oom: Afrikaans for uncle.

Sies! An Afrikaans expression, universally used by English and Afrikaans speakers in South Africa, to express disgust. English speakers pronounced it 'sis'.

Ossewa (Sg) and Ossewaen (Pl): Ox wagons used by the Boers, the Afrikaans farmers and pioneers, as transport. Equivalent to the covered wagons used in North America, and drawn by oxen

Poep: Afrikaans for feces, used in expressions such as in "I'm poep-scared" of something or someone.

Rara avis: Latin expression meaning rare bird, an odd or eccentric person.

Rhodesia: The former name for Zimbabwe.

Rubber: An eraser

The San: The sanatorium, the school sick bay, presided over by Matron.

Scone: What North Americans call a 'biscuit', only much more delicious!

Snoek: Afrikaans word for a type of fish, regarded as a delicacy when eaten as smoked snoek.

Sonde met die Bure: Title of Afrikaans book, meaning "Sins against the Neighbours" or "Trouble with the Neighbours."

Shongololo: An insect resembling a centipede that would curl itself into a circle if touched.

Sosaties: Afrikaans word for kebabs, in general usage.

Stompie: Afrikaans word meaning cigarette butt, in general usage. *Taal:* Afrikaans word meaning language.

Taalpuriste: Afrikaans word meaning language purists, the people who fought to purge anything 'foreign', especially English, from the language.

Tokoloshes: Evil spirits, feared by Africans.

Two-way: A very tight elastic corset, used for flattening your stomach and your behind.

Veld: Afrikaans, The Bush, in general usage.

Veldskoen: Afrikaans, literally 'Bush shoes', soft-sided shoes made out of suede, sometimes referred to as 'brothel creepers'.

Voortrekker: This Afrikaans word is difficult to translate exactly. It has the connotation of travelling away from a place. The Voortrekkers were groups of Afrikaner farmers and their families who, in the 1830s and 1840s, were the first to 'trek' (depart) from the Cape Colony to explore and settle the hinterland to the North (later the South African provinces of the Orange Free State, the Transvaal and Natal). Their principal objective was to depart from the British-controlled territory and to form independent self-governing communities. They travelled in ossewaen and on horseback.

Vrot: Afrikaans word, pronounced 'frot', meaning rotten.

ABOUT THE AUTHOR

Catherine Kentridge was born in Johannesburg, South Africa. She grew up there, attending private all-girls' schools. After she matriculated, she went to England to an all-boys' public school, where there were a few girls in the Sixth Form. She intended the time in England to be a gap year before returning to South Africa to study at one of the universities there. Instead, the time in England turned out to be a turning point.

Catherine was offered a place at Oxford University to read English Literature. After Oxford, Catherine studied law in Chester and London, very surprised to find herself beginning to follow in the footsteps of her advocate parents. She quickly discovered that law did not suit her at all, so she returned to South Africa where she became an editor and then a journalist.

Catherine emigrated to Canada in the early 1980s and has lived there ever since, working for many years as a journalist, broadcaster, and editor. More recently she has become a storyteller, and a wedding and memorial service celebrant. She lives in Toronto. Catherine is the daughter of the distinguished South African and international lawyers, Sydney and Felicia Kentridge. Most of her family now lives in England: her parents, her sister, Eliza, an artist, and her brother, Matthew, an international management consultant. Her brother, the artist William Kentridge, continues to reside in South Africa. Catherine is working on two novels, one for children and one for adults.

www.ingramcontent.com/pod-product-compliance
Lightning Source LLC
La Vergne TN
LVHW021447080426
835509LV00018B/2191